Healing the Folks Who Live Inside

Healing the Folks Who Live Inside

How EMDR Can Heal
Our Inner Gallery of Roles

Esly Regina Carvalho, Ph.D

2012

Healing the Folks Who Live Inside: *How EMDR Can Heal Our Inner Gallery of Roles*

ISBN: 13:978-0615795904
ISBN-10:0615795900

Cover: Cássio Eduardo Moraes Barbosa and Joelton de Oliveira de Souza
Photograph of the author: Selma Pikcius
Illustrations: Esly Regina Carvalho, Ph.D.

Special thanks to:
- Tamara Dusek who made this English text so much more readable.
- André Maurício Monteiro who encouraged me to use my own drawings.

Esly Regina Carvalho, Ph.D.
SEPS 705/905 Ed. Santa Cruz sala 441
70.080-055 Brasília, DF Brazil
info@plazacounselingservices.com
www.plazacounselingservices.com

Table of Contents

Presentation

This book is the result of a thirty-year career of psychotherapeutic work. My initial training was in Psychodrama and Group Psychotherapy. The first time I put my foot on a stage, I fell in love with it. I remember saying to myself, "Self, you were born to do this thing." And so began a psychotherapeutic love affair that has not faded. I studied everything I could in Brazil and the United States, and was eventually accredited as a Psychodrama Trainer (Trainer, Educator, Practitioner, USA) and Trainer/Supervisor (FEBRAP- Brazilian Federation of Psychodrama, Brazil). Eventually I began the Psychodrama movement in Ecuador in 1990, which resulted in an Ecuadorian Association (APSE) that continues to train group therapists.

Fifteen years after learning Psychodrama, I discovered EMDR as a client. It changed my life - both personally and professionally. I walked out of my first EMDR session in 1995 determined to learn it. In 1997, I finished my basic training under Francine Shapiro, Ph.D., the brilliant developer of EMDR, and was later trained and accredited as a Trainer of Trainers through the EMDR Institute and EMDR Ibero-America due to the efforts of John Hartung, Psy. D. I feel privileged to be part of the EMDR team that trains in Brazil, Latin America, and the Iberian Peninsula. By 2012, we had trained more than 1,200 EMDR therapists in 15 cities in Brazil alone.

During my wanderings around the globe, I also met Carlos Raimundo, M.D., an Argentine-Australian psychiatrist and psychodramatist who developed the work of Play of Life™, a micro-stage Psychodrama/Sociometry approach that allows us to study and treat the roles we play in life. It is a method of specifically identifying our inner roles and their interactions with one another.

I am deeply grateful to each member of the Outer Gallery of people who have influenced the development of my work and the emergence of this book. My life and my work are better because of them. So now that you have met some of them, let's talk about the Inner Gallery of Roles – the folks who live inside each of us.

Preface

All of us have "people" who live inside. If we stop to listen, we can hear the "voices" of many of them. Sometimes we hear the voice that says, "You are so stupid!" when we make mistakes; *Scaredy-Cat* is afraid of everything and prevents us from doing a lot of worthwhile things out of fear. Some of the "folks inside" are so anxious that they cause us to make bad decisions just so we can put an end to our feelings of anxiety — when instead, we should be solving problems with prudence and wisdom. And, all of us have an *Inner Medical Doctor* ...

Every day the Inner Gallery is present in our lives. They start developing very very early! We can easily become aware of some of our roles if we stop and listen on the inside. However, there are other roles that govern our lives without us ever realizing it. The one who sits in the "driver's seat" of our lives is the one who often makes the decisions. If our Inner Child takes over the decision-making process from the Adult who should be in charge, we may wind up with more problems than solutions.

Once, I had a patient who asked me if I thought she would be able to spend a month in another country in order to perfect a foreign language. I told her:

"It depends ..."

"Really? What does it depend on?"

"It depends on who goes ..."

"I'm not sure I understand what you mean...?"

"If the capable and mature Adult Engineer goes, I think there will be no problem studying abroad for a month. But if your seven-year-old *Inner Child goes, the one who lives tied to her mamma's apron strings, you'll be back in 24 hours ..."*

"Oh, I think I get it..."

It doesn't take much to become aware of some of our roles, but there are others that we will have to pay attention to (or enter therapy) in order to understand them. Many times, when we do not understand why we do certain things, it is likely that some hidden role kidnapped the one who should be in the driver's seat of our lives, and took over our actions.

In Brazilian homeopathy it is said that the difference between medicine and poison is the dosage. The same thing goes for our Inner Gallery. In some extreme cases, we find people who have developed different "personalities." (We'll discuss this later when we talk about dissociation). They often navigate life without any awareness of other parts or roles. Even when confronted with the reality of their actions, they cannot remember what they did when they were in another role. This is a rare situation, although more common than previously thought. What is common is to have our gallery populated by roles that were blocked in their development when we were growing up.

In recent years, the emphasis of my work has been to help people heal from trauma and painful memories. The more I work with this issue, the more I am convinced that traumas-big and small - are affecting our lives today. Those traumas impact our ability to choose wise responses and to react well to the daily situations we face. In a sense, we were made for a perfect world, and we really do not know how to deal with imperfection, violence, death, the breakdown of interpersonal relationships, disappointment, or the loss of our dreams and our hope for a better future.

I hope this book will clarify the existence of our Inner Gallery of roles, explain how these roles are born and develop within you, and help you understand what function they have in your life through their interactions. Finally, I trust this book will provide you with ways to heal those wounded characters of your Inner Gallery — those characters that prevent you from living life to the fullest. You can learn to celebrate those roles that edify you, lift you up and serve as positive resources for your life. This will happen when you learn to negotiate a "good neighbor policy" on the inside, amongst the roles that live within you, your Inner Gallery.

Introduction

This book was written for the general public as a way of helping people understand themselves better. It can help people make contact with their inner roles: the folks who live inside. For this reason, the language is simple and, hopefully, accessible to all.

I would like to clarify from the outset that I do not think the roles that represent our Inner Gallery are real "people" inside of us, but are only a creative concept used to help us understand our inner roles and how they guide our thoughts, emotions and behaviors. These are internal constructs that all of us have.

Psychotherapists in general can take advantage of the therapeutic concepts presented here, and will no doubt identify the steps of the professional protocols, but Psychodramatists and EMDR therapists will especially benefit from the procedures and case stories presented here. Those who want to understand what EMDR and the Play of Life are all about, may want to skip the beginning of the book where trauma and its consequences receive the major emphasis. This might help professionals understand some of the case observations presented in the early chapters.

The cases presented here are true, but care has been taken to disguise all identifying information. All names and personal details have been changed to protect the identity of people who have shared from their lives. These situations took place around the globe, since I have lived and worked in four countries, and have treated people in many more.

I have always chosen a different name to describe a specific case, but it is impossible to avoid the use of common names. Nowhere was the actual name of a patient used. My clients (past and present) can be assured that if they find a case with a name like theirs, they are not the subject described in the vignette. Any similarity between the names of my clients and the cases presented is purely coincidental.

The essence of these stories has been maintained in order to illustrate how the new reprocessing therapy, EMDR, can change people's lives especially when aligned with earlier theories and practices like role therapy and Psychodrama. Unfortunately, the emotional feel and the physical expressions of patients is somewhat lost in the writing, but I still believe that it is possible to get an idea of how the session develops, as well as to understand the speed and impact of EMDR.

That said—let's get to know the folks who live inside?!

Introducing the Folks Who Live Inside

All of us have "folks who live inside." These are inner roles or "folks" that develop over our lifespan, many of them during childhood. These roles have certain elements in common:

1. **First of all, this inner gallery of roles really does exist, but only inside of us.** *Newborn Baby, Inner Child, Adolescent in Crisis, Teenage Rebel, Scaredy-Cat,* our own *Mother* and *Father*, or the *Inner Medical Doctor* are all roles that may have come to live within us as a result of our life experiences.. Each time an incident in our life was "poorly digested" or "filed" away in our brain in a maladaptive manner, one more of these roles became frozen within our psychic (neurochemical/brain) existence: as a new addition to our Inner Gallery of roles. This is the result of normal development and it should not surprise us.

Emily: *I have the feeling that many people live in here ... the way you described the Inner Gallery of roles. There is a Scaredy-Cat ... she reminds me of a frightened kitten. When she shows up, I get butterflies in my tummy. I panic. I don't think I can deal with the simplest of situations. When the Adult reappears, I can't understand how that Scaredy-Cat could be so frightened about such a silly little thing, something that was so easy to solve. But when Scaredy-Cat puts in an appearance, there is nothing I can do to calm her down. I think maybe she just needed a hug from someone who cared about her...*

Lana: *I have a Weeping Willow inside. You know, that tree that has long branches and seems to cry beside the river...? That's it. There is a Weeping Willow that lives within me. She is about 13 years old. She told me that where she lives inside there is not a single solitary adult nearby who cares for her...*

2. **The Inner Gallery of roles also exists inside of other people.** Have you ever had the experience of talking to someone when you suddenly get the feeling that you are no longer talking to the same person anymore? Perhaps your friend or loved one gets angry beyond measure, or throws a jealousy fit. or suddenly becomes cold and calculating, or begins behaving like some 3 year-old?

Beth said to me, with a smile on her lips, *Can you believe that when I got back from this last trip that the little brats that live inside of my husband all came out to see what I had brought in my suitcase - and began to complain that I had brought more gifts for other people than for him!*

3. **Wherever we go, we take our Inner Gallery with us**. The problem is that sometimes these inner folks show up seemingly out of nowhere, and they may be scared, or angry, or totally lost. Their unexpected appearance can keep us from doing things that are important to us.

It took me a long time to understand that mortgages are just paper, said John, during a session. *Every time I had to deal with these issues of paying rent, bureaucracy and paperwork, bank loans, all these kinds of paperwork I would go into a total panic. I made poor business deals and even sold a house abruptly, because the anxiety associated with these processes kept me from making good decisions. During a session with EMDR therapy, I was able to get a grip on the Child's anxiety and transform the "bureaucratic disaster" into an adult reality scene. I came from an immigrant family, where we had to learn a foreign language at home and all of us were lost trying to make sense out of the culture. Most of the time we were all buried under mounds of information that made no sense to us as foreigners. Sometimes at school, I caught the words spoken to me, but I could not understand the meaning or context. When I finally realized it was one of my Inner Kids who would come into play every time I had to deal with this stuff, I began to assure Little John that loans were Big People stuff and that I, the Adult John, would take care of it all. Bank stuff wasn't for children. I will never forget going to the bank last week and saying softly to myself, "John. Bank mortgages are just paper.*

That's all they are. They are just paper. One paper after another... just paper..." I was finally able to do the paperwork without an anxiety attack.

4. **Our Inner Gallery of roles was formed from the inter-relationship with other people: roles and counter roles.** As we grow up we "introject" (put inside) aspects of the personalities of those with whom we live. We develop our role as *Mother* based on what our mother was like, even though we swear we will never be like her or do things like she did. We develop an *Internal Mother* that has a lot to do with the external mother who raised us. When we have children, we are likely to imitate many of the things that we learned from our external mother.

Marilyn sighed and said: It's time to return to my external mother all of those things inside of me that I have been dragging along in my Inner Mother. I see now why it is so hard to make decisions! When I was growing up, every time I decided to do something, my mother would make an issue out of it. Now I realize who it is that complicates my decision-making process. It's my Inner Mother. So... today I have decided to give back to my external mother everything that belongs to her. This stuff doesn't belong to me. From now on I am going to decide these things ... just me and myself and nobody else.

In the Inner Gallery of our lives there is also that *Internal Mother* who still "speaks" and triggers things inside. She is part of the roles that have formed within us and have become part of the Inner Gallery. Our external mother may have died 20 years ago, but she can still be alive and well in the Inner Gallery.

In an EMDR session with Maria, she said that she had had a very critical mother who never gave her any praise or positive words. The first memory she had, at age four, was her mother accusing of her having done something wrong. I asked Maria to step into the role (role-reverse) of that four-year-old *Inner Child*, and we started processing those memories with EMDR. As Maria tearfully commented that the mother always said such critical things, I told her that all of us have a volume button, and that she could adjust the volume regarding what her mother said or even put it on mute. After a series of EMDR bilateral movements, she said:

"But children have to - must! – listen to their mother's voice!"
So I said:
"But you can choose what to hear."
Thinking it over, Maria replied:
"You mean that I can use a filter? And I can choose to hear what is good for me, and not listen to what hurts me?"
"You can now…"

5. **The wounds of the Inner Gallery can hurt the Outer Gallery.** Traumas are like splinters in the heart of each person. These splinters can hurt others. Every time we approach other people we can hurt them with our splinters (and their splinters can hurt us, too!). Have you ever tried to hug a porcupine? Well, there are some people whose Inner Gallery is so full of splinters that every time they try to embrace each other, they hurt more than they love…

6. **Our Inner Gallery also has positive roles.** Many people who are considered "strong" or resilient were able to develop Inner Gallery members who helped them overcome the challenges of life. Some people had enviable childhoods and have naturally acquired a positive role repertoire. Others managed to develop an Inner Gallery of positive roles despite their circumstances. Some had a significant person in their life who invested heavily in their emotional growth as an individual. Or perhaps they were born with a temperament or an inner disposition that allowed them to overcome adversity. The truth is, that to a greater or lesser degree, there are positive roles inside each of us. Thus, one of our psychotherapeutic tasks should be to help clients heal and develop positive members in their Inner Gallery.

Rose once told me, "*I remember that in the midst of the chaos that was my family, I had a sewing teacher during my adolescence. For four years I went to her class every afternoon. Sometimes I was upset because my mother told me I could only do the course on the condition that I also sew for my sister. It really angered me because when I made a special dress, like for the prom ... I was in despair, trying to finish both my dress as well as my sister's! It was all so unfair! But Mrs. Jones would help me. She was patient with me, and would explain things to me, and now I realize that those classes were an oasis of stability in my life as a teenager. She appreciated me. I still do things the way taught me. Sometimes I even wonder what she would do in a given situation...*

7. **We can learn to listen to our Inner Gallery.** All of us have these inner dialogues with ourselves, between our Gallery members. As we learn to pay attention to what they say, their needs, why and how they were formed, and what they need to calm down and live better, -we will have a healthier life. Learning to listen to ourselves is a great gift. If we are taught to pay attention to others, why not learn to listen to ourselves?

When I was a teenager I felt the same as Ugly Betty, remember her? Eyeglasses, braces on my teeth, hair tied back in a ponytail ... I felt like I was a foreigner in my own life, an observer, not a participant. Now that I listen to myself I realize that I'm beautiful! Many of the things I appreciate today (like classical music, poetry, and literature) were things that my Teenager taught me. Today I am very grateful to her ... I see that I'm beautiful!

8. **Because these roles live within us and are the fruit of our perception, we can change their content.** We should not think that we are forever doomed to live bound to and trapped by an unhappy childhood. Nor should we fear that the experiences that plagued us our whole lives must continue to hurt us in the present. The perceptions of our Inner Gallery members can change, and as a result, we can be free to make new choices and look at other options. We can make decisions that bring us health, personal fulfillment, and greater satisfaction with life.

Jennifer: *I remember when I was a lanky pre-teen and we went to a party. While we were still in the car my uncle and the other children made fun of me. I was so upset with what was happening that I got out the car. I went home on foot. I felt like a baby, abandoned on the side of the road. I was really hurt with all that happened. Can you imagine that my mother, who was also in the car, let me do this?!*

The therapist told Jennifer that she could now redo the scene in ideal terms: the way she would have liked for it to have happened. After reprocessing with bilateral movements of EMDR, Jennifer said:

But now I see that I, the Adult can rescue this girl who is in need of parental protection (BLMs[1]). In addition, I remember my mother commented that she - my mother - had also been ridiculed during her adolescence (BLMs). Now I can do things differently. I can tell my lanky teenager what I wanted my mother to have said, "You are my dear and precious daughter, and I will go back with you." Ah! I see my mother going back with me, so that I did not have leave alone. I feel defended and protected (BLMs). I hold no more hatred. I understand what happened: she was a victim just like me (BLMs). She told my uncle that we were no longer going to the party. She and I went home, talking along the way. She stopped at a store and bought popcorn and candy, and we went home together.

9. **Our Inner Gallery members can change addresses.** They are not forced to live forever in our past in their original form. We can rescue them from where they live within us and bring them to the present. We can heal them, and give them what they missed (fill what are often called developmental deficits, or emotional "holes" that appeared due to the lack of emotional satisfaction or fulfillment). Now, our *Inner Adult* can be the mother or father we longed for when we were growing up. They can instruct our present lives with wisdom or innocence or joy. We are not condemned to live in the past that did us so much harm. We can seek out our seven-year-old *Inner Child* and take it out of that disastrous home. We can go for a walk in the zoo of our inner present. It is a matter of perception ... and perception is everything. How we do this is part of the purpose of this book.

---

[1] BLMs – Bilateral Movements done in EMDR

The Metaphor of Trauma: Remember Lot's Wife

One of the best metaphors about trauma comes from the Bible. It is an ancient story and well known to those who study the Judeo-Christian Scriptures. The story goes like this (Carvalho version)[2]:

Abraham, the father of the Jews, had a nephew named Lot. Both of Abraham and Lot prospered, and their herds of goats and sheep grew to the point that their servants began to argue about pastureland. So that there would not be disagreements in the family, Abraham proposed to Lot that they separate and go in opposite directions. Lot could choose first. Lot agreed and eventually went to live in a city named Sodom. According to the Biblical narrative, God decided to destroy this city; but since God promised Abraham that He would not destroy the just along with the unjust, God sent an angel to warn Lot and his family to flee the city. Lot took the angels home with him, thinking they were human beings, and the angels then warned him. Part of the divine message was that neither Lot nor his family members should look back as they fled. They were instructed to keep looking forward until they reached their final destination.

The men Lot's daughters were engaged to didn't believe this message. They thought it was all a big joke, so they stayed behind while Lot, his wife and his two daughters ran off toward the plains. Lot and his family hadn't gone far when the skies began to rain sulfur on the city, but they huddled together and kept running. All of them, that is, except for Lot's wife. For some unknown reason, she looked back and when she did, she became a pillar of salt!

This is the metaphor of trauma. In a certain sense we can become pillars of salt, eternally frozen, looking back at where the

---

[2] The original narrative is in Genesis 19:1-29.

tragedy and destruction are happening, instead of moving forward. We can't see things as they are in the present, nor can we run toward the future by fleeing from what is happening. Trauma causes part of us to remain frozen, looking back at death and destruction, (neurobiologically speaking as well). Our brains get stuck "looking" at the past. We drag these statues of salt along throughout our lives, and whenever we try to do something to resolve these inner situations, the terrified statues start yelling and screaming! They can only see death and destruction. They cry out, "Look out! Danger! Danger! If we try to resolve this it will be a disaster!"

One of the interesting aspects of this is the recent scientific studies that confirm and explain how these memories really do get stuck and frozen within the memory networks in our brains. This is not just a metaphor that imprisons people. Brains really do mediate and store memories in mal-adaptive ways which are disconnected from precisely those parts of the brain that could help "digest" and process these painful memories. We can even see this in sophisticated brain scans: the traumatic memory is stuck in the brain without resolution in much the same way that the pillars of salt are stuck ever looking backward at tragedy and destruction.

The truth is that people were created for a perfect world and have never gotten used to evil or imperfection. The traumas of life break us all and when this happens, little "pillars of salt" or inner roles are formed within us. We spend the rest of our lives dragging them along until the day – if it ever arrives – when we are finally able to visit these memories and melt them. How does this happen? Among the important elements that can help people heal is the therapeutic relationship where these statues can be "embraced" and melted by love and compassion. There are many techniques, suggestions, and therapeutic approaches that will bring about this melting, and some of them will be presented in the following chapters. But in ultimate analysis, what really heals is love - mediated in a relationship of protection, safety and attunement with the other person. It is love that will finally melt the interminable winter of the statue trapped in its vision of terror and destruction.

Trauma and Its Consequences

Trauma hurts people in many ways ... more than most people imagine. It is not just the "obvious" traumas that hurt, such as kidnappings or rape, war experiences, urban violence, earthquakes, tornadoes, floods or hurricanes. Trauma can also include those painful and adverse experiences that do not necessarily fit into psychological diagnostic categories. "Light" traumas can also leave us with painful consequences.

For example, a patient mentions the fact that every day during his childhood and adolescence his father criticized the way he ate at the dinner table: He would spill his glass of milk, drop his fork, or handle his eating utensils improperly, His father thought his comments at the table were stupid ... and today the patient complains that he has a hard time going out with his friends to eat. A beer he can just barely handle, but a sit-down meal at a restaurant? No way! It is never any fun. Just the thought of of going out with his friends provokes enough anxiety to make his stomach turn, his heart take off, and his body break into a cold sweat.. This patient cannot be classified as someone suffering from Post-Traumatic Stress Disorder (PTSD); but nonetheless, these memories definitely limit his daily life.

So let's talk about the consequences of painful experiences and memories, and how discuss how they can affect our lives:

1. **Trauma freezes memories at a neurochemical level in the brain.** Recent studies with brain scans (such as CAT, PET, SPECT scans, MRI, etc.) show how dysfunctional information can compromise brain activity. There are parts of the brain that contain memory information stored in maladaptive manners.

Susan sighed deeply and said, *"I am an Ice Heroine. I solve everybody's problems, but ever since all of that happened to me, I am paralyzed when it comes to solving my own problems..."*

For Susan, the "frozen" parts do not communicate with the functional parts. Sometimes the traumatized individual doesn't even have words to explain what happened to them because traumatic memories tend to be stored away in the right hemisphere — and words are in the left, which is the hemisphere of language and logic. When the hemispheres are not "talking" to one another there isn't a way to attribute meaning to what happened. The maladaptive information is dissociated from the tools that could help process and resolve the bad memory

Selena shared with huge sadness: *I had a little sister who was born much later than the rest of us. Soon after I became pregnant with my first child, my little sister passed away. When she was seven years old, he caught one of these childhood diseases that were common in my country. Back then there were no antibiotics or medicine that could cure these things. My mother was never the same after that. She used to dress up in silks and pretty jewelry. She would go to the beauty parlor every week and have her hair done. But after my little sister died, she never dressed up like that again ... never wore her jewelry and never went to the hairdresser's anymore. She started wearing her hair up in a bun like the little old ladies ... she never got over my little sister's death.*

Selena's mother didn't have the tools that would have helped her resolve the traumatic memories left by her daughter's untimely death. What she needed was to reprocess and adaptively integrate these experiences into her brain. This type of brain-based reprocessing happens in psychotherapies such as EMDR. By creating new connections in the brain, the memories are transformed through adaptive information, insights, and perceptions, all of which lead to resolution.

Elaine said: *I turned my Little Girl loose so that she could play inside in a safe place. It had been years since I felt like this! I used to be a doll made of plaster.*

There are studies that hypothesize that trauma is more of a sleep disturbance than one of memory dysfunction (Stickgold, 2007[3]). There are parts of our brains that process information even while we sleep. This is a normal function of the sleep cycle: We dream, we process and "digest" what happens to us, and we put it away in an adaptive manner. When traumas are formed – they are organized as memories that are often dissociated or disconnected in a maladaptive manner, and as a result, the brain is no longer able to perform its normal function — that of processing

[3] Stickgold R, Walker MP. *Sleep-dependent memory consolidation and reconsolidation.* Sleep Med. 2007 Jun; 8(4): 331-43.

information during sleep. In some extreme cases, the memories that are not processed adequately become dissociated memories that can't even be recalled under normal circumstances. So we often have situations where even our sleep is not able to resolve our traumas because the processing mechanism is "stuck." The result is that we have nightmares, and bad dreams, and we wake up startled. Sleep does not repair nor restore like it should. Instead, it's as if we spend the whole night trying to resolve inner conflicts, but to no avail. We toss and turn in our beds, but do not progress down the path of resolving painful memories because this mechanism is "frozen."

3. **Trauma is the result of dangerous experiences (either real or perceived) that we are unable to adequately resolve.** It is known that when we face dangerous situations we react in one of three ways: fight, flight, or freeze.[4] When a fox finds a rabbit in the woods, the rabbit is instantly aware of the fox and must react or will become the fox's dinner. If the rabbit is trapped, he will fight, since he has no other options. If he thinks he can run faster than the fox, then he will flee. But sometimes, when the rabbit is on the run, and the fox is gaining on him, he will freeze. The rabbit will fall as if dead, in a physiological state that will make the fox think he really is dead. Since dead meat is of no interest to the fox, he will leave the rabbit, and depart for better dinner possibilities. When the rabbit realizes that the danger has passed, he will begin to tremble and shake as he comes out of this frozen state. If he doesn't emerge from the trauma just right, the risk is high for him, because he may quite literally "die of fright." However, if the rabbit comes out of this frozen state properly, he will see another day, and live free, without the consequences of trauma.

Human beings also have many of these same reactions. Remember the pillars of salt? They are a good example of the inner roles that we have been unable to properly "shake off." The experience doesn't "go away" and the danger is felt as if it is eternally present.

---

[4] See Peter Levine's book, *Waking the Tiger*, for a more detailed explanation of this phenomenon.

The wise author of Ecclesiastes says that God has put eternity in the human heart (Ecc: 3:11). In a certain sense this "eternity" is the unconscious mind that has no sense of time. Unhealed traumatic experiences eternally repeat themselves inside of us. This repetition doesn't end because the brain stays actively connected to our unprocessed memories. Our brain stays in a state of hyper vigilance because the deep brain continues to feel the need to protect itself from perceived danger. It is as if our internal mind doesn't "know" that the danger has passed, so it continues on high alert, in an anxious state, always concerned that something bad is going to happen. Somebody inside continues to live and relive the traumatic experience...

My sister told me this weekend that the neighbor we had when we were young (who was so strange) had lost absolutely everything because of a lightning strike to his house. Everything burned. He had a bunch of kids, and he lost everything... the house, the harvest, the horse ... everything. She said that the neighbor was never the same after that.

4. **One of the things that trauma does is take away our capacity to choose.** We were created to choose freely. If we are healthy it implies that we have the ability to choose how to respond or react. Trauma takes that away from us, and obliges us to repeat unwanted behavior or responses. This may help us understand why certain people repeat destructive behavior even when they know better, and even when they don't want to. (Who doesn't know a woman who has been caught in a violent cycle of behavior? Perhaps earlier traumas keep her from breaking off this destructive relationship.) Sometimes it is worth going back to examine these patterns when we see that some of our behaviors have begun to "freeze up." Pillars of salt do not offer us healthier behavior alternatives.

5. **Trauma makes us believe lies about ourselves.** One of the things that happens when we go through a painful experience, and are unable to properly process it is that our memory maintains the same pain, thoughts, smells, sounds, and colors that were attached to the original experience. These elements stay connected in a "package deal" within our brains. The thoughts are often irrational and false. They are the lies we believe about ourselves as a result of painful unprocessed memories. There is a

part of us that knows all of these byproducts aren't true, but there is "somebody" inside of us that went through the experience and continues to "see"destruction. This somebody can no longer believe the truth about what happened-the truth, that the experience is now over and there is no need to hang on to the painful associations connected to these memories. Unfortunately, pillars of salt do not believe our adult self.

Leticia: *I just don't think that I am an interesting person. Ever since that happened to me when I was ten years old, I think that I'm ugly, I'm poor, and that no one would ever want to be with me. I'm already 40 and I'm still unable to find someone to marry me. My relationships don't last very long, that is ,when I finally am able to get a boyfriend. The truth is that I don't believe I deserve good things...*

For example, sometimes women who were raped at gunpoint know (rationally) that if they didn't go along with what the rapist wanted, their very life would be in danger. But there may be a part of those women, the "someone" who says, "It's all my fault." They think ... "What if I had done this?" or "Maybe if I hadn't done that?" or "Maybe if I had gone down a different road that day ... or stopped for coffee ... then this wouldn't have happened ...".

That's the lie...

Believing the truth means that woman did the best she could to survive and not get killed. We need to help people like this melt the lies so they can believe the truth that will set them free. But that doesn't happen through the application of rationality or logical arguments. Lies get resolved through the reprocessing of trauma in our brains.

One of the important and little-known characteristics of traumatic events is that people actually have normal reactions when facing abnormal situations. For instance, it is abnormal to be assaulted, raped or kidnapped; however, it is normal to feel absolutely terrified and for a long time after the event, fear that the danger hasn't passed. Sometimes people's brains are able to "digest and metabolize" these events spontaneously due to their inner resources and resilience. But this doesn't always happen, and that is when the frozen state becomes more likely. To have these "inner statues" as a result of such experiences is common, but it can be limiting. Sometimes our brains are simply not able to process the enormity of what happened. Bessel van der Kolk[5], states that the difficulty of dealing with trauma is facing the truth of what has happened: It means dealing with the truth and its enormity.

6. **Trauma came impose obsessive and intrusive thoughts.** In the aftermath of trauma, we just don't seem to be able to stop thinking about what happened. It bothers us on a daily basis. I say to myself, "I'm not going to think about this anymore. I'm going to change my subject matter." And sure enough, a few minutes later, there it is again! And I catch myself thinking about it once more.

It is difficult to deal with intrusive thoughts. We finally feel at ease for a few minutes, then all of a sudden thoughts from our past come back to haunt us. We didn't call them up. We weren't even thinking about the experience, but still, the thoughts intrude. Sometimes it is more subtle. We don't understand why our mood has changed or why we suddenly got sad for no apparent reason. Or perhaps we got irritated without cause. What's happened is that something in the present has tripped the "Past Button" and someone in our Inner Gallery of roles has come to pay an unexpected (and usually unwelcome) visit.

7. **We develop avoidance behaviors**. Difficult experiences make us want to avoid "that" again. If something traumatic happened on a certain street corner, then we find a way to avoid that corner. If a bad experience happened at a certain restaurant, perhaps a last fight that ended our marriage, then we will never want to eat there again. The problem really becomes evident when the avoidant behavior begins to generalize and we avoid an ever-growing number of places, things, and even people.

That's how phobias begin. We have a bad flight experience, and we don't want to get on an airplane again. We present in front of an audience, and some folks snicker and make fun of the way we speak or dress so to avoid the risk of

---

[5] Van der Kolk, B., McFarlane, A., Weisaeth, L. (1996) *Traumatic Stress: The Effects of Overwhelming Experience on Mind, Body and Society.* New York: Guildford Press.

embarrassment and humiliation we don't ever want to speak in front of people again.

Priscilla: Whenever I get on an airplane I feel little and scared. I need someone who is stronger and bigger than I am. I curl up into a little ball ... I know that I need to be logical and rational about this, but I just can't! It seems like there aren't any adults to accompany me on my trip ...

Therapist: But a little girl can't travel on an airplane by herself! She needs an Adult. Where is the Adult who can accompany this scared little girl?

P: I have the feeling that there isn't anyone!

T. Tell the little girl that there is an adult that always goes with her whenever she travels – your Inner Adult! And she can always hold her hand. Think about that, and follow the movements.

8. **Our capacity for learning is affected and often blocked**. Traumatized people have trouble learning. There doesn't seem to be space in their brains for new information. and they lose the emotional ability to learn. People often think that those who have been traumatized are dumb or stupid. They may not have done well in school. When I ask them what their life was like back then they give me a long list of problems they were facing: humiliations at school, parents who were separating, lack of support and guidance, and so on. I explain to them that with this level of "inner noise" there really isn't room for learning. It's not that they lack intelligence. It's just that they just weren't able to listen to the outside lesson because the inner noise volume button was turned up so high. When we help people heal the inner noise, we open up the space for real learning. The pillars of salt were taking up the space for algebra.

9. **Trauma opens the door for evil.** What does this mean? In simple terms, violence generates violence. That's not to say that some people are simply bad or evil (we admit that psychopaths do exist), it's just that when we look at some people's lives, they tend to be full of traumatic stories of violence, exploitation, injustice, abandonment and negligence. It is not necessarily a coincidence that they are on the roster of the bad guys or *bandidos*. They just may not know anything else. The good

news is that if we can help heal the kindergarten of inner children the "bad guys" carry around as adults, we may have the chance to rescue the good that is also inside of them. It may not always be possible, but it is worth a try--especially if that person is willing to pay the price that comes with emotional healing.

10. **Life breaks us all but some people become pillars of salt.** All of us have some places inside of us that have frozen to the point that those places are lifeless and resemble a pillar of salt. Once again, it is a dosage issue. The more roles that have been frozen, the more limited becomes our life experience. Life is not fair in its distribution of traumas and painful experiences. How each of us deals with these experiences will depends on who we are, what is involved in our life story, what our temperament is like, and what psychological development (or developmental deficits) have been created by our family context (or lack thereof).

11. **Life also breaks those who watch the tragedy**. We are not only traumatized by what happens to us, but we are also traumatized by what happens to others. We easily forget that first responders, like medical staff members, firemen, police officers, military personnel, and others who live on the front lines, are also impacted by the tragedies that happen to others. We may take someone to the hospital, witness a car accident, violent shooting, war scene, or natural disaster. The list is endless. It is very difficult to watch a child die, or to sit at the bedside of someone who begs to be saved, then passes away. Vicarious suffering can also be traumatic. Compassion takes its toll on those who are confronted with so much disaster, violence and suffering. People helpers can be traumatized by what they experience on a daily basis. Compassion fatigue can set in because for all of us, there is a limit to how much tragedy we can handle.

12. Finally, we need to understand **that without healing for the heart there is no quality of life.** Imagine trying to live an uplifting life while dragging around these inner pillars of salt! The more we heal, the more integrated are the members of our inner Gallery, and the greater quality of life, we enjoy. Maybe that is the best reason to seek the emotional integration of our Inner Gallery of roles? When our inner life is integrated, we can make better

choices. We can respond more adequately to the challenges (and people) that come our way. We can enjoy the goals we have achieved. Most importantly, we can fully love and let ourselves be fully loved.

Trauma steals all of these good things away from us. When we cure our Inner Gallery, we reclaim that which is most essential and important for the human being: the ability to live in a relationship of love and mutual respect – within ourselves and toward the outside world as well.

Role Theory

My thirteen-year-old daughter has Down's Syndrome. Like most adolescents, she tries to get around the rules, and even though she knows she can't pull it off, she insists, and challenges our agreements. When I confronted her about one of these situations, she answered:

"But, Mommy, I didn't do it. It was just one of my thoughts. Really and truly, it was my brain!"

I replied: *"But your brain is part of you!"*

She answered: *"Then we will have to talk to this brain so that it doesn't get me into these difficult situations because otherwise I get punished..."*

So, we "talked" to her brain and they *"made an agreement"* *(her words)*. Now they work together so that she can do what she likes without breaking the rules!

Role theory was developed in a revolutionary manner by Jacob L. Moreno, the genius who created Psychodrama. He would say that roles are cultural units of behavior (Garrido, 1978). Roles possess particularities and characteristics of the culture in which they develop. The word *role* comes from the Greek *rollo* which referred to the scrolls that were wrapped around a cylinder for drama/theater presentations. They were primitive books from which actors memorized their parts.

We can also say that a role is a "dynamic structure within an individual, based on needs, (beliefs and values) that come alive under the influence of a social stimulus or in definits positions"[6]. The manifestation of a role is based on the expectations an individual has with regard to him/herself and others, as well as his/her interaction with certain groups and situations.

---

[6] Munich and Astrachan, 1983, p. 20 – Group dynamics, in H.I, Kaplan & B.J. Sadock (Eds), Comprehensive Group Psychotherapy (2nd edition, pp, 15-23) Baltimore: Williams and Wilkins in Gladding, S.T., 1999 p. 59. *Group Work: A Counseling Specialty, 3rd Ed.*, NJ:Prentice-Hall.

I realized that I always seemed to have two extremes in my life: very good or very bad. I wound up becoming very pessimistic and always looking at the bad side of things. The good side would be forgotten. For example, I have the image of an Abandoned Child, but there is also the Beloved Child. There is a Neglected Child, but the Studious Child also exists. I would eat compulsively during my adolescence but I developed a Healthy Eater who really knew how to deal well with food. And then there's the Timid/Quiet/Introvert, but the Extrovert shows up as well.

Every person is born into an existing culture or social network. That cultural reality is defined both personally and collectively. We can say that a role is a tangible way of being. It is not the person's self nor is the person him/herself. This means that if we want to define the self in some experimental way, we need to resort to the roles they play.

According to Moreno, the self is born from the roles and not the other way around. This means that we will spend our life integrating these roles that are constantly forming so that we can acquire a greater and greater sense of an integrated self. That is why we have the experience of an Inner Gallery: These are the roles that speak and act within us and that we should try to integrate more and more through an inner "policy of good neighborhoodliness." For us to be happy our inner roles need to get along with one another.

Moreno said that we develop our roles by playing the roles. We begin with psychosomatic roles, i.e., those that have to do with indispensable physiological functions, such as eating, sleeping, urinating, etc. Later on, little by little, we begin to develop social roles that correspond to the individual's social functions and through which s/he relate with his/her surroundings. These roles emerge as a result of the identity of the groups to which we belong (family, school, work, etc.) In ideal terms, we develop more and more social roles, such as that of daughter, brother, kindergarten student, nephew, grandchild, and eventually our adult roles: student, professional, mother/father, chauffeur, teacher, etc. Our inner roles emerge as a function of our counter-roles – how I relate with the people around in my family, school, etc. The counter-role is the complementary role: daughter/mother, student/teacher, boss/employee, and so on.

Who I am has a lot to do with what others are like, and with what they teach (father and mother), or transmit through life experiences (school, work, friends, etc.)

Finally we have what Moreno calls psychodramatic roles, and these are the roles within our imagination. We can "be" Superman, Ideal Mother, Fashion Model. We can also be those roles in which we role-reverse: I become My Mother, My First Grade Teacher, My Inner Doctor, etc.

The number and characteristics of these roles depends on the availability of roles. For example, a person who was raised on an old-fashioned farm may have less access to social roles than someone who was raised in a modern urban center. This is what we call the "repertoire of roles." It is the "list" of different social roles that we possess in life.

When we have lots of roles, we talk about richness or variety of roles; and when we have just a few roles, we see a certain scarcity or poverty of roles. The importance of having a variety of roles has to do with the flexibility we need to face life situations and to develop a more appropriate understanding of others.It is also important to be able to understand that there are a variety of roles that we will never acquire, such as president of a country, astronaut, or a Nobel Prize winner.

Every person has multiple roles that they develop and play in life. When a group or an individual changes, their roles will often change as well. This is one of the wonderful things about working with people's roles: We do not have to be tied to certain roles all of our lives, nor do we have to be tied to how we developed them (neither quantity nor quality of roles). It is possible to change how we play these roles as we pursue a greater quality of life. We can acquire new and better roles (through a healthy Inner Adult), and we can play them better in life in ways that are more productive and appropriately matched to who we have become as we heal.

We spend our lives learning roles. No one is born knowing all of this. This learning process is important because some roles are essential for our survival. Some have to do with issues of life and death, like knowing when we are in danger, taking care of babies and small children so they can survive into adulthood, knowing how to find food, how to work and provide for ourselves, and how to manage reproductive roles. Roles need to have social adequacy and appropriateness. They need to be developed and played functionally within our circle of life and relationships. It is also important to remember that what works in a social role in one culture does not always work in another culture. Other roles emerge and are born of the experiences we have gone through in life (a divorcee only learns that role having gone through a divorce.)

I wanted to tell you a little bit about the metaphor that came up spontaneously without having thought about it before. Like I told you, it was very difficult for me to have gone from a state of being healthy to one of being sick. Going from health to sickness was like an emigration: like going from one country and arriving in another. I had to leave behind the security of all that was familiar to me and the sense of belonging to a certain group of people – the healthy – and all of a sudden my reference points changed. The chemotherapy room, where I went three Fridays a month for four hours was transformed from a strange, distant and faraway place that was so threatening, into a roomful of welcome and comfort where people understood me and what I was going through. The folks who stayed behind – in the country of those who were healthy – became distant. With few exceptions, I no longer felt understood there. When I would try to relate to them or when I would come up from my own inner world where the anguish of death battled the hope that things would turn out well, I would connect with people who would inundate me with well-intentioned advice. Sometimes this would offend because they seemed to want to know more about my situation than I did, as if not only was I sick but ignorant about life.

The other country was the one I used to live in, to which I would return after gadding about in my new life. You know what they say... when one goes away, one changes, and the ones who stayed behind also change. There were some people who always remained close by, who did not think they knew more about me and my sickness than I did, who would listen to me patiently, who knew how to console me, how to just be with me. I have friends who know how to be in all of my worlds, my countries with me, and even though it is difficult for them, they humbly try and often succeed in their efforts.

Nowadays it isn't so hard being sick... it is a reality I can face. I don't know how it happened, it just did, and the world of before now seems distant. I'm not sure I really know what I want with my life. I'm in a kind of state of immanence, where what matters is only the present day, this moment, and what can come of it right now.

Another interesting aspect of role theory is that roles are not the general personality of the person. For example, because a woman is an architect does not mean that she only sees herself as such. A person is much more than a single role they play in life. One cannot be reduced to just a professional role. My professional colleagues can identity with the experience of sitting next to someone on an airplane who finds out I'm a psychologist and says, "Oh, I need to be careful about what I say or you will analyze me!" What they don't understand is that when I am sitting on a plane, reading a book, I'm not in my professional role. Nor do I spend my life analyzing (and judging!) everyone around me. I have many other roles besides this one.

However, it may happen sometimes that people have trouble separating themselves from the roles they play. This can happened with adults that come from dysfunctional families. They may continue to play certain roles they acquired in their childhood, such as adult children of alcoholics, where they continue to play the roles of *Hero, Scapegoat, Lost Child* or *Clown*[7] even after they no longer live at home. Unfortunately, in such circumstances people can become trapped in certain roles or interactive patterns to the point that this hampers them in all of their relationships. This is why it's so importance to identifying the roles we play in life, so that we can evaluate if that is how we want to live for the rest of our lives.

When we talk about the impact of trauma on our roles, we need to remember how trauma "forms and freezes" roles. *Remember Lot's Wife.* When something agonizing happens to us –

---

[7] Harris, S. A. & MacQuiddy, S. (1991). Childhood roles in group therapy: The lost child and the mascot. *Journal for Specialists in Group Work*, 16, 223-229; and Wegscheider, S. (1981). *Another Chance: Hope & Health for the Alcoholic Family*. Palo Alto, CA: Science and Behavior Books.

and it may be a big or little trauma, one that we may think didn't leave any sequelae, such as a father's rebuke – we sometimes form new roles from the interruption of the normal development of our life roles. "Someone" inside our Inner Gallery of roles was formed or had their development stunted as a result of these experiences. That is why different roles have different ages and emotional content: They were frozen and trapped at a certain point in our development. Sometimes we even feel fragmented as a result of so many broken roles inside.

Chuck Pierce[8] talks about how oftentimes, "we are fragmented in our soul with pieces of our life scattered here and there... parts of the whole person that we should be lie scattered along the paths of our lives."

If we understand that trauma breaks us all, then we also understand how this fragmentation forms our inner roles. For example, sometimes people say that they are sabotaging their lives. They say they know that they need to do such-and-such (or leave off doing it), but they feel helpless when it comes to changing their behavior. According to role theory, we can understand that this is due to the fact that there is a part that is frozen in time (dissociated) and that this role can no longer jump on Life's Bandwagon and accompany the Inner Gallery.

It is important not blame the victim. When we speak of self-sabotage, manipulation, or behaviors that lead to secondary gains, it is important to remember that there really are inner roles that are not able to pursue the train of life. It's not that they don't want to; they just can't. We need to be careful not to overburden people who already feel and perceive their limitations - one more members of our Inner Gallery of roles needs to heal, get over their fears, be reassured that they are safe now, acquire new abilities, and permit a greater and better integration of their roles. When these roles get healed they automatically change, and the person is able to begin to reach their goals in life.

We need to learn how to negotiate a healthy way of living together amongst our Inner Gallery of roles, heal the wounds, and

---

[8] Newsletter, July 22, 2010 by Chuck Pierce, cited with permission.

pain that are held in some of these roles and melt the frozen pillars of salt. Each part or role contains information, aspects and content that contributed something to the person's personality and the integrity of their self. This perspective should fill us with hope since we know that we are no longer obliged to live in a fragmented or dysfunctional manner. We can change our roles both in quantity as well as in content. Hope comes from the fact that we are no longer condemned to repeat difficult histories, but can now find new solutions to old problems by healing our inner roles.

Sharing from the Inner Gallery...

What follows is a small portion of a therapeutic session. Watch how Annabelle finds her Little Ballerina and with it, her femininity. This portion of a session exemplifies how we can "rematrix", that is, re-edit the old dysfunctional pathways through a therapeutic relationship. It is very important for every human being in the course of his or her development that they can be seen and confirmed in their existence through love. Sometimes the therapist is the ɹirst person who accomplishes this in aa person's life.

Since there is no sense of chronological time in our unconscious mind, even if the reparative process occurs in the present, the Inner Child of the Past can hear and receive this confirmation in the present. This can heal and validate that which was not received or that which was lost in the past. David Grand[9] once commented that the Child Within us has to hear what it needs from our Inner Adult and not necessarily from external figures (whom they don't always trust or believe). All of this is inside of our brains: healing the Inner Gallery, changing our perception of the past, inner conversations with our roles, etc. What is inside of us is what needs to change – and can change – because we can change the perception within our brains.

Partial report of an EMDR session

Annabelle shares about a childhood situation that still bothers her and we set up the EMDR steps in order to reprocess with bilateral movements. There is silence between each set of bilateral (eye) movements Annabelle shares a little after each set. The total time for this session is much longer, but what follows is only the relevant part of the session.

A: *I still feel trapped in that childhood scene. I am not able to disconnect from that set of images. It still affects me as a person. I feel insecure. I am a woman without strength.* (Bilateral movements = BLMs)

A: *Now I have been able to calm down the Little Girl that feels*

---

[9] Brasilia, April 16, 2010, personal communication

she is in danger. I took her by the hand and took her out of that scene. She goes out a door. (BLMs) I feel more emotional. (BLMs)

A: *How funny! When I was little, I loved ballet! Some of my happiest memories are of me dancing, dressed like a ballerina. (BLMs) I just realized that I limited my feminine side because I always thought this aspect of me was linked to violence. I don't even dance ballet anymore. I think I became afraid of the violence against women after what I witnessed growing up at home. (BLMs)*

A: *Now I feel better. I think I finally understood. Maybe I dissociated all of this. I need to go back to ballet classes urgently! I have a feeling of being free, of having freedom inside of me!*

Therapist: *I have a proposal. Let's watch this Little Ballerina dance?*

A: *YES!! Let's do that!* (Therapist and Client look at the EMDR light bar, and together they "watch" Little Ballerina go through her steps. (BLMs) *That was just great! I am free, without worries. My Little Ballerina was dressed in pink chiffon. I'm fine, and she is really happy, proud of herself. Hmmm, there is a lack of more love in this scene... for myself... (BLMs) Oh! I... I love myself! I am a good person! I saw this little five-year-old girl. We are in communion. I love her very much. I tell her that I love her, and that everything is going to be all right, that we are all right. Now I don't have any disturbance when I think about all of this. I believe that I am loved. I love myself! I feel that I am really recovering this little girl and her femininity.*

T: *And what does of this mean for you today, as an Adult Woman?*

A: *I am a complete woman. And I... am going to sign up for dancing classes...!*

The Inner Gallery of Roles and Dissociation

Most of us have had the experience of driving along the road and becoming so absorbed that we miss our exit. Or sometimes we "get distracted" and the car goes somewhere "on automatic." Sometimes we are far away while the teacher is talking, and we don't remember what she said while we were daydreaming. All of these are examples of "normal" dissociation.

The truth is that there is such a thing called "adaptive dissociation." When we have to do an MRI (Magnetic Resonance Imaging), there is no good reason why we have to believe that we are inside of some huge steel cigar with only an inch of breathing room, while we put up with the procedure. Instead, the whole time we can think that we are on a beautiful beach, where the sun is shining, and where we are listening to the ocean waves break. This is a healthy way of dealing with a difficult situation.

As we said earlier, the issue of dissociation is a matter of dosage. When our Inner Gallery begins to lose awareness of the existence of some of its members, then we may need to start thinking about unhealthy dissociation. The "borders" of our roles may get more and more rigid and compartmentalized, and there may be less flexibility and awareness amongst the roles.

This may be a serious disorder that requires professional help, and oftentimes medication, in order to deal with the long and winding process of healing. People who have Dissociative Identity Disorder (once known as Multiple Personality Disorder) have a series of limitations that can complicate their everyday life. Oftentimes they have gaps in their memories and can't remember large parts of their childhood, or other parts of their life. Sometimes they don't seem to remember how certain things happened, or that they held certain kinds of conversations, and the amnesia for some of these roles can be pretty all-encompassing. How something happened while they were in another role is an unknown since they do not have access to the content in that role because it is dissociated from that experience. Until more recently, many people believed this only happened in the movies. But the truth is that many of these dissociative disorders are more common than once thought and they often turn up in the therapists' offices. Perhaps diagnosing it properly is more uncommon... and that is one of the psychotherapeutic problems, since not all professionals have learned to diagnose it appropriately.

In the Inner Gallery, certain experiences get "dissociated" as our life goes on. That is one of the ways that some of the members of the Inner Gallery develop. The inner role becomes an aspect of the Gallery that didn't develop on purpose, but came about as a strategy in order to protect us and help us survive. My friend, Silvia Guz[10], says that dissociation is like when a breaker drops and the circuitry gets switched off. In the same way that the light switch stops the flow of electricity in order to avoid a fire, the person dissociates in order to avoid an emotional heart attack.

No one has a totally integrated personality. The concept of the Inner Gallery is a normal manifestation of roles that develop inside all of us. But when there is an extreme disconnect between these roles, where some experiences are completely blanked out, then we are probably looking at more serious cases of the dissociation spectrum. In these cases, it is like parts or roles are more rigid and are present in different and independent forms, as if they had a life of their own. In these cases when the roles are rigid and not very porous, in some theories these roles can be called "alters." In such cases, usually at a much slower pace, the therapeutic task in very simplistic terms is to find a ways that these roles (or alters) can become aware of each, heal their past emotional wounds, and learn to walk together in harmony instead of pulling in different directions. The idea is to make it possible for them to lead a more normal and integrated life. But because of the severity of some of these cases, we often measure the therapeutic improvements in millimeters.

It is common in traumatic dissociation for there to be a total disconnect between consciousness and experiences. In our brain, the event remains dissociated from the neuronal resources that could help process these memories. That is why traumatic

---

[10] Personal communication, March 20, 2011, São Paulo, SP, Brazil.

experiences often feel like they are still in the present, when in reality, they happened years, or even decades ago. Because it is dissociated, it is hard to remember. The flip side is that oftentimes when memories are retrieved, they come back like a flood. When we work with people with dissociative disorders, we are looking at people who are very fragile, and yet very strong since they were able to survive such terrible tragedies. People have to be allowed to remember at their own pace in order to avoid re-traumatization.

Some people develop these disorders as a result of chronic and ongoing trauma, such as incest or physical abuse, experienced during childhood. They often describe living their lives as on "automatic pilot" or in a "cloud." They often have time distortions or lose track of time altogether. Some folks can't even remember what they did during the day.

This kind of dissociation can manifest itself in many different ways. (Haddock, 2001:2) They are unaware or can't control their dissociative responses, which often occur in inappropriate situations. The intensity and duration of the dissociation can severely limit people's daily lives.

It is important to remember that dissociation is an emotional defense that protects people when they can no longer tolerate the emotional suffering that they are going through. It is a survival strategy, but the spell has fallen back on the wizard: dissociation "protects" from the emotional pain, but it also keeps the experiences from being processed by encapsulating or compartmentalizing it in the brain. It disconnects the suffering from the neurobiological (and emotional) resources that could permit its adaptive resolution.

How strange... today my eyes are tearing up so much... I don't understand why, said Peter, innocently, *as he dried his eyes with the tissue paper.* We had been working on an especially difficult situation in his childhood.

Therapist: *Maybe your eyes are tearing up because you are crying? Maybe they are tears of mourning?*

P: *Do you really think so? That I am crying? (as he dried more tears with the handkerchief).*

People who struggle with dissociative disorders should not be embarrassed or ashamed of this. The dissociation fulfilled a very important function in their life at critical points. It is not an exaggeration to say that were it not for the dissociation that they might have died of an emotional heart attack or they might have been led to a suicide attempt in order to dull the pain of the traumatic experience. The problem is that once the traumatic experience is no longer happening, and the threat is over, the dissociation then interferes in the daily life of the person. In this sense, dissociation becomes a mal-adaptive strategy for life in the present.

With the new therapeutic approaches that reprocess painful and traumatic memories such as EMDR, therapists are more able to help people deal with dissociation in a way that allows the memories to integrate in a healthier fashion. However, dissociative disorders need to be treated by specialists in this field, those who can accompany these clients. Not all of these cases are indicated for EMDR, and many clients will have to do preparation work in order for the person to be able to submit to this kind of therapy. However, within the dissociative spectrum, many do respond well to reprocessing.

EMDR – Eye Movement Desensitization and Reprocessing

Tamara got up from the table, took a deep breath and went up the escalator for the first time in her 58 years of life. Helen arrived at the office and shared about how she had been able to have an MRI without any anxiety or medication. Rodrigo went back to driving his car for the first time since the car accident that took his friend's life. Patricia was able to have blood exams after losing her fear of needles. John's commented on the experience of having his house burglarized and six members of his family held at gunpoint for four hours, an experience that had him so incapacitated he hadn't been able to work for a year: *"Oh, that's just a story to tell at happy hour."*

EMDR

What do all these people have in common? They have submitted themselves to a new and revolutionary approach called EMDR – Eye Movement Desensitization and Reprocessing - which was discovered in the United States by Dr. Francine Shapiro in 1987. Since then, more than 100,000 therapists have been trained worldwide in EMDR, which represents a paradigm shift in psychotherapy.

If we understand that traumas, nightmares and bad memories of adverse situations are stored in a mal-adaptive form in the brain networks, then we can begin to understand how EMDR can reprocess these fears, phobias, terrors, and anxieties that are connected to painful memories that keep victims trapped by these ghosts from the past. This is accomplished by the integration of reprocessed information that was once in separate parts of the brain. In an accelerated and adaptive manner, EMDR seems to "imitate" what happens to people as they go through the REM (Rapid Eye Movement) phases of the sleep cycle. This is the phase when the brain processes daily life and stores it in an adaptive form, then transforms it into past memory. For reasons that are not totally understood, in some situations people are not able to process this information in a normal and healthy manner. Perhaps this is the origin of nightmares, startle responses, intrusive and obsessive thoughts, or post-traumatic stress disorder (PTSD) and its consequences. In some cases, people can develop Dissociative Identity Disorder (DID) as a result of chronic, repetitive and constant traumas (such as incest) that occur during childhood.

In order to apply EMDR, the psychotherapist needs to have been duly trained in accredited courses, where both EMDR theory as well as the practice of the eight phases of EMDR therapy are taught along with three-pronged (past, present and future) protocol. Trained therapists learn how to evaluate the indication (or lack thereof) for EMDR therapy; how to develop a treatment plan; and how to conceptualize the diagnosis and treatment according to Adaptive Information Processing which is the theoretical basis for EMDR. Beginning with the first phase, the patient shares his or her history, and the therapist then identifies the adverse situations, traumas and painful memories that may become targets for future reprocessing. In the second phase, the therapist will help the patient install positive resources that will help the patient face difficult moments within or outside the sessions. Different kinds of bilateral stimulation (visual, auditory and tactile) are offered to the patient so that he or she can become familiar with it. In addition, the EMDR approach is explained to the client in order to obtain informed consent. In the third phase we "open" the brain file that contains the difficult memory by asking for the image, beliefs, emotions and sensations that are tied to it.

EMDR therapists use two measurements scales. The first is the SUDS (Subjective Units of Disturbance Scale) which measures disturbance. Therapists will often ask the patient, "On a scale of one to ten, where ten is the greatest disturbance that you can imagine, and zero is no disturbance at all, how much disturbance do you feel when you think about that experience right now?" This allows the therapist to accompany the level of resolution of the experience while the bilateral stimulation is being applied. This scale was originally developed by Joseph Wolpe who worked with desensitization and developed the means to evaluate subjective experiences statistically.

The therapist also uses a second type of measurement when asking the client to think of an ideal situation in which the present experience has been totally resolved. The therapist then asks, "On a scale of one to seven, where seven is completely true and one is completely false, how true do you feel the positive belief about this experience is to you when you think about it?" This second scale was developed by Francine Shapiro, making it possible to accompany the resolution of the traumatic experience as it is processed and becomes more and more adaptive in nature.

Because of these measurements, it is possible to develop statistical designs for empirical research. Perhaps one of Dr. Shapiro's greatest contributions has been her insistence on research which has led to the publication of over 200 scientific studies in peer-reviewed journals, and to a journal dedicated specifically to EMDR Research and Practice[11]. In 2010, EMDR was recognized and acknowledged as an evidence-based psychotherapeutic approach by the National Registry of Evidence-Based Programs and Practices (NREPP)[12]. Nowadays, EMDR efficacy is undeniable.

In the fourth phase, the therapist applies the bilateral stimulation that helps the brain reprocess the painful and/or traumatic memories. The bilateral stimulation re-activates the Adaptive Information Processing system which was previously unable to fully process the experience and therefore stored the information mal-adaptively. EMDR gives the brain a second chance to reprocess the traumatic memory, thus transforming it into an adaptive resolution.

Oftentimes, people will have intense emotional reactions when reprocessing. This should not surprise us, since past experiences come up much in the same way that they had been stored. This does not mean that the person is being re-traumatized. It simply means that the negative content is being discharged.

---

[11] http://www.springerpub.com/product/19333196 retrieved March 16, 2013

[12] http://nrepp.samhsa.gov/ViewIntervention.aspx?id=199 retrieved March 16, 2013

On the other hand, intense abreactions can reach a tipping point since it is no longer an issue of reprocessing because the client may dissociate and the processing stops altogether. The person's brain becomes unable to make the adaptive connections necessary to take the experience to an adequate resolution. We can say that with over-the-top emotions, some of the Inner Roles get scared and "flee" (dissociate again) to their frozen places in order to protect themselves. Through dissociation they go to the place where they have the illusion of being protected (and pay a high price for this). But the survival strategy once again converts the situation into an ice cage.

Each traumatized role has aspects that are frozen and dissociated. When the client connects to this role, it triggers all that was stored away dysfunctionally. Oftentimes, what is triggered are roles that were frozen in childhood, a time when the person had fewer resources, options or choices regarding how to deal with what was happening to them. Their "emotional circuits" got overloaded and dissociation was how they survived.

The fifth phase begins when the negative and painful memories have been reprocessed, because then positive beliefs can be linked to the target memory the client is working on. It is as if the patient, having emptied out the glass of dirty water, can now fill that glass with clean water.

In the sixth phase, the clients does a mental scan of his/her body and determines if there is any physical disturbance left in their body, which is also processed with bilateral stimulation.

The session ends with the seventh phase, in which the client is given specific instructions about what to expect between sessions, how to contact the therapist if necessary, and how to take note of what happens to them during the coming week.

Finally, the eighth phase occurs when the client returns for the next session, and the therapist receives his/her feedback and evaluates the results from the previous session. This information will help guide the therapist concerning how to proceed with the treatment plan.

As always, an appropriate history-taking is essential in order to evaluate whether the client has an indication for this kind of psychotherapy, since there can be contra-indications. Although the results can be amazing at times, these are not "miracle cures."

In order to process effectively, it is necessary for the patient to feel safe and secure. A great part of this security comes from the therapeutic relationship. If it is not possible to trust the person who will accompany us on this healing pilgrimage – and there may be terrifying parts on the road – then patient will not surrender to the healing process. After all, there is a whole gallery of roles for whom the Adult feels responsible--roles that need protection. If any of the inner roles don't feel safe and protected, or if they get scared, or feel frightened, the process will not move forward.

This is one of the reasons why we emphasize that what heals is love. Perhaps it sounds strange to talk about love in a psychotherapeutic context, but it is love, positive affect, and unconditional positive regard that will give clients enough security and a sense of safety so they can find the courage to board the ship of hope and stay onboard till the very end. It is the security of unconditional acceptance on the part the therapist that will encourage the patients to take this trip inside of themselves to visit the members of their Inner Gallery. Getting to know the wounded members of their Inner Gallery will allow them to be healed with these new psychotherapeutic tools; but without love, no one has the courage for the trip.

What is it about EMDR that makes it seem like a paradigm shift in psychotherapy? First of all, it is an approach which produces brain changes. Modern brain scans[13] demonstrate the physical changes that result from the application of EMDR. The resolution of the painful experience is the result of the integration of neuronal information that is often dissociated in the brain networks where the traumatic information and the resources for healing are stored in separate hemispheres. Sometimes clients say that they "don't have words to explain what happened", and this

---

[13] Lansing, K., Amen, D., Hanks, C., Rudy, L. (2005) High Resolution Brain SPECT Imaging and EMDR in Police Officers With PTSD. *The Journal of Neuropsychiatry and Clinical Neurosciences* (17) 4.

is literally true because the unprocessed memory is dissociated from the part of the brain that can attribute words and meaning to what they have experienced. Only after it is reprocessed can the client report an integrated explanation to their experience.

Secondly, talking about their negatives experiences is not necessary for clients to heal. For 120 years psychotherapists have been taught that patients must talk about their painful experiences in order to change (beginning with Breuer's revolutionary "talking cure"). However, with EMDR, talking can be kept to a minimum, since what will heal the patient is the reprocessing of the memory in the brain. For some clients who are shy, or too embarrassed or too ashamed to talk about some of their experiences (such as sexual abuse or rape), this aspect of EMDR is a godsend. It allows clients to reprocess their memories in private.

Perhaps the greatest joy we have as EMDR therapists is to hear our patients, when they have finished reprocessing their memories, tell us things like...

"It's over. Now it's distant. It's in the past."

And when they come back in the following sessions they say:

"I remember, but it doesn't bother me anymore."

"I can't remember it like I did before."

"It's not clear and crisp anymore. The picture is cloudy."

"Is it normal to have so much relief in such a short amount of time?"

"People say and do those things that bothered me so much before, and now, it doesn't matter anymore."

"I'm sleeping well for the first time in years!"

"Hmm. ow strange. I haven't thought about that at all during the week."

"Funny, this EMDR stuff... It's like it never happened to me. It's like the EMDR put that experience in a place where it never happened. It's like I used to look at a room filled with old stuff and now it's all gone. Everything is organized and I can't even remember what it was like before!"

"This EMDR is magic...!"

EMDR Session

Claire came to therapy because she wanted to resolve some issues from her childhood. She commented on the fact that when she was little, she and her sisters would hear their mother having sex in the next room She was aware of the fact that during a certain phase of their lives, they were so very, very poor that their mother took up prostitution in order to provide basic care for her children. Claire's mother had no formal schooling, was completely illiterate, and had been abandoned by her husband (their father) with three little girls. This was the only way she had been able to make ends meet, since she was a foreigner in that country, and didn't have her family of origin to fall back on.

Claire talked about how difficult it was for her to go to sleep. She had insomnia and attributed it to the fact that she would often get frightened at night when she was little, awakened by the noises coming from the next room. She would get so anguished by it all that she couldn't get back to sleep. It didn't seem to affect her sisters, but as the oldest, she worried that something bad was happening to her mother.

As we set up the EMDR session, Claire stated that she wanted to work on this scene from her childhood. The image was that of Claire in her bed, with the pillow covering her ears, with a cold pit in her stomach, and with the fear that something bad would happen. Her negative cognition was, "I'm unprotected", and she wanted to be able to believe fully that "I'm cared for." Her Validity of Cognition (VoC scale) measure was five (on a scale of one to seven). Her feelings were that of sadness, fear, insecurity, and a level of disturbance on the SUDS scale of seven (on a scale of zero to ten). She felt cold sweat and goose bumps all over her body.

After three sets of eye movements Claire said that she could no longer hear the sounds that bothered her so much at the beginning of the session, and she no longer had anxiety or fear about the memory. She said her level of disturbance had fallen to zero.

When I asked her about the positive cognition, she said that several things had changed. That now she could see the positive side of what had happened.

"The truth is, my mom was an overcomer, a heroine. She struggled so hard to provide for our survival, for our basic needs, clothing, food, and studies. For a time, this was how she was able to make ends meet."

After a few more sets of eye movements, Claire shared about how her mother had later been able to get a job as a maid, and had completely left that kind of life. And after a few more sets of eye movements, Claire told me that neither she nor any of her sisters had ever gone down that route.

Visibly relieved, Claire said she couldn't understand why this didn't bother her anymore. She commented that she was afraid that the anxiety and fear might come back. I told her a little bit about the Inner Gallery of roles, and proposed that her Adult speak to the little six-year-old girl who had lived inside her all this time. Perhaps she could tell the little girl that now her Inner Adult could care for the child since this child only really existed inside of the Adult Claire.

Claire closed her eyes while we changed over to tactile movements on her hands, and when she looked at me again, she said, "I went and talked to the Little Girl because she was scared of going to sleep and risking hearing those sounds again. I told her she didn't need to be afraid anymore, that it was over, and that everything had ended well. I also told her that I, Claire Adult, would take care of her while she slept, and that way she would be well cared for. It's funny... I saw that my sisters were sleeping calmly, that they were OK. And that's when my Little Girl rolled over and went to sleep while I watched over her as she slept."

With these new insights into her childhood experience, Claire said that her belief in her positive cognition had moved to seven (totally true). She could now believe that she was being cared for, since her Adult could now fulfill this function in her life.

"I had never seen the positive side of all of this before. My mother was a woman who went out and fought hard in life for our survival, and it saddens me to think that she had to pay such a high price for it. This was how she was able to accomplish such a huge task back then. But she did it because she loved us, so she could provide for us. She cared enough to want to give us a better life than the one she had. We never went hungry nor did we lack for the basics in life. She was a real heroine."

I asked Claire to think about that childhood scene once more, and she said, "I went back into that bedroom and all three of us were fast asleep. I'm glad I was able to explain things to the Little Girl, because now she knows she can sleep peacefully."

It never ceases to amaze me how quickly and how adequately a response can come out of our clients' brains. Claire resolved a situation that had disturbed her since early childhood, and she did it in one session. At the beginning of the session, she shared how ashamed she was to even tell me the story about her mother; but when we finished, she said she was even proud and admired her mother for what she had to do to care for her daughters.

Play of Life: Finding Out Who Lives Inside...

The *Play of Life* was developed by Dr. Carlos Raimundo, an Argentine psychiatrist and psychodramatist who immigrated to Australia during the 80s. The *Play of Life* is based on the theory and practice of Sociometry and Psychodrama as developed by Jacob Moreno, the brilliant Austrian medical doctor who grew up in Vienna and was a contemporary of Freud's. Moreno immigrated to the U.S. before the Second World War.

The *Play of Life* kit is a practical means of placing thoughts, ideas and internal situation in a visual, dynamic, concrete and external forma. It is a kit with miniature dolls (Playmobil®), three stages and some objects that permit the visualization of relationships, roles, and relationships. It offers clients the opportunity to look at alternatives and changes that can give them a chance to look at things differently and find a better future (Raimundo, 2000).

According to Raimundo (2000:1) there are several goals that can be reached through these exercises:

- It permits the client to see how emotions are affecting them since we can put them "outside" on the external stage.

- It transforms verbal (uni-dimensional, linear) information into visual information (tri-dimensional).

- Clients can visualize how they perceive themselves in relationship to others.

- Patients can look at present situations and rehearse changes and alternatives knowing that they can go back to the original setting if the changes are not satisfying.

- Clients can photograph or tape the scenario so they can take the new possibilities with them.

In a very singular and clear way, the *Play of Life* gives us the opportunity to concretely visualize our Inner Gallery of Roles. We can "see" externally what goes on internally. Through the *Play of Life* we can give "voice and life" not only to our inner roles, but also to our emotions, feelings, illnesses, alternatives, dreams, and possibilities. In the hands of a capable psychotherapist, it is possible to identify, diagnose and treat the Inner Gallery of Roles. As we listen to the complaints, needs, and dreams of our inner folks, we can begin to think about how to give them what they need, heal their wounds, dream together, and allow them to grow up into an adult life of emotional integration that will lead to ever greater health.

Session with the *Play of Life*

Leonard commented at the beginning of the session: *"I am always starting over, with the fear that everything is going to go wrong."*

Therapist (T): *"How about we have a look at what is going on in your Inner Gallery of Roles? It seems like there are some folks there who are not all playing on the same team, and that this is getting in the way of your success."*

We set up the *Play of Life*[14] and I asked Leonard to look inside and identify the inner roles (the members of his Inner Gallery of Folks) and lay them out the way he felt that they were organized inside of him. *"Place your roles according to who plays on what team, here and there."*

Leonard picked up one of the dolls that had a coat and tie, and placed it on the little stage, looking out. Then he took a little girl dressed in pink and said, *"This one represents my childhood."* Finally, he took a red bearded doll in a police uniform and placed it with his back to both of the others. "Childhood" was between the two, looking in the same direction as Coat-and-Tie Leonard, a little behind him. *"She is further back, but not against them."*

Regarding Coat-and-Tie Leonard, he said, *"This represents who I am; gray, in a suit, serious, in a more responsible way."*

About Policeman Leonard, he said, *"He's like a policeman, red, with an angry face and a rebel way about him, like I was in my adolescence. He represents the Frustrated Leonard. I always feel frustrated with my decisions, my attitudes. It seems like my head and my emotions are totally different one from the other. I always did poorly in school. I would like to go back into the past, and live that all over again,*

---

[14] Developed by Carlos Raimundo, MD. A small kit with three mini-stages, Playmobil™ dolls is used to discover, understand and modify aspects of people's relationships. See www.playoflife.com

but make different decisions. Honestly, I'm scared of starting this new project and only getting halfway through it once again.

T: *"Leonard, did you notice that the two 'Leonards' have their backs to one another?"*

L: *"Yes, I wanted to move forward and the other kept looking back, to what I was, to what I wasn't. There is a saying that if you always look back you will never see what's in front of you. You wind up falling into a hole. I would like to be able to accept what has been, and to know that what I am going through now has nothing to do with what happened, but I can't. I would like to be able to see a little bit of happiness on the way. I'd like to be able to move forward, without looking back, because if there is a hole, I'm going to fall into to, and when I fall, I will need a lot of time to get myself back up again.*

This Policeman only wants to look back. He doesn't see the present or the future. He looks back, at a past that he will never be able to touch. I would like to go back in time and do everything different, but I can't. I'm afraid to look forward. My past is tragic, but at least I'm familiar with it."

T: *"These dolls represent elements in your life. Here you can change whatever you like because all of what you describe exists, but only inside of you."*

L: *"Can I change dolls?"*

T: *"Of course. Here you can change whatever you want, rehearse it, and if you don't like it you can go back to what it was like before."*

Leonard chose a blue doll with a hat. He took The Policeman out and placed the blue doll looking forward at Childhood and Coat-and-Tie Leonard.

L: *"I chose a funny-looking doll because it represents my funny side. I think that this might be the first way to solve the problem. I'm going to take my inner clothing of rage and rebellion regarding my relationship with the world and that the Policeman represents, and transform life into something a little lighter."*

T: *"Great! Because if you continue with this Policeman inside of you, you will continue to fail. Failing is what he knows how to do best, as you have realized. If things don't change, when you grow up (the therapist said jokingly) you will be this loser that you have just described... very much like your father, whom you described here in therapy, as a loser. You learned the lesson well with him and can consider yourself well on your way. It is really wonderful that you are willing to try something new, something that will help you look forward, and who will play on your team."*

(Leonard picks up the blue doll and places it next to the doll that represents his childhood.)

L: *"I carry a huge emotional concern, I'm absurdly worried. I don't know if this is going to work. I'm trying to be more aware of things, because I'm unpredictable even to myself. I would really like to be able to start this new project, and study, but I have this fear that at the first obstacle I'll give up. I'm beginning to trust who I am now, but I don't trust who I was."*

T: *"I think you are right in not trusting the Policeman. He looks backwards and doesn't see the holes. I don't suppose it's worth growing up and being like him!"*

Leonard was silent... thinking... and reprocessing while he looked at the stage.

T: *"It's funny, while you were describing this blue doll, it reminded me of a cowboy. I'm not sure why..."*

L: *"Wow, I was playing this video game about the American Far West, and there was this guy who liked to fool around, but then he becomes this cool guy. I've made a lot of mistakes in my life, but now I wanna get it right. This Cowboy (and he points to the blue doll) is trying to fix things with more self-confidence. What do I do to become like that?"*

T: *"You need to choose. Now you can choose, if you want to be like this Policeman – and you know that life all too well – or if you want to try and become more like the Cowboy, lighter more trustworthy. You choose minute by minute, then hour by hour, then day by day until it all becomes automatic, and the Cowboy becomes a part of you, more than the Policeman. Maybe it's time to have a marathon session of Far West movies? And pay attention to the cowboys; see them as a better model than the Policeman?"*

L: *"Wow, I never realized I could choose..."*

Play of Life y EMDR: Negotiating the Inter-Relationship of the Inner Gallery

Pauline arrived at the session very discouraged about her weight. She had put on about 25 pounds in the last year and a half, and she knew she needed to lose weight. There was an important wedding coming up in eight months and it was important to her to be thin and to participate in a pretty dress.

So we decided to work with the *Play of Life*, so that she could identify what roles were in conflict within her. She identified the following roles: Fatty, which was how she felt right now. And the Future Thin Me, which was how she wanted to be, so that she could travel and attend her best friend's wedding in another country. (See the photograph.)

Fatty (white figure in the middle) and Future Thin Me (purple figure on the right)

We set up the traditional EMDR phases, with the image, cognitions, emotions and physical sensations:

Initial image = Fatty (white figure) sitting down
Negative Cognition of Fatty = I can't control myself
Positive Cognition = I can control myself
Validity of Cognition (VoC) = 2
Emotions (as she looked at Fatty) = anger, sadness, fear
Level of Disturbance: SUDS = 9
Physical sensations = in her tummy and thighs

Using tactile bilateral stimulation while Pauline looked at the scene where Fatty and Future Thin Me were placed, the reprocessing phase went like this:

Pauline/Fatty thinking out loud:

"Other people manage to go on diets. I'm a bunch of pounds overweight." (BLMs). *"Others can lose weight but I can't."* (BLMs). *"It's not fun to have to zip my mouth. I love eating, but if I let things slide it will be worse later on."* (BLMs). *"I started gaining weight when I didn't have time to eat right at lunch. I began eating out and quit exercising."*

Therapist [T]: *"And now, when you look at this scene, how much does it bother you on a scale of zero to ten where zero is nothing and ten is the most that you can imagine?"*

Pauline [P]: *"Fatty? 5, but if she lost some weight..."*

T: *"What would you like to say to Fatty?"*

Pauline: *"Fatty, you need to zip the lip, join the gym, exercise more willpower, and control the sweets."* (BLMs). *"Fatty, you have already started... I can eat less. I can avoid repeating portions."* (BLMs). *"Yesterday I sat next to someone who eats a lot, and I was able to wait till the end of the meal without repeating and no desert."*

Measuring the level of disturbance (SUDS):

T: *"So, now on a scale of zero to ten, where ten is the maximum disturbance that you can imagine, how much disturbance do you feel now when you look at Fatty?"*

Pauline: *"It's a three, because until I can see myself skinny it bothers me. Until I get rid of this belly, it's hard to say that I'm OK."*

Since the level of disturbance didn't come down any more because of a reality issue (she really hasn't lost weight yet), we looked at other factors that might be contributing factors.

T: *"Let's talk to Future Thin Me? Remember that your Positive Cognition is, 'I can control myself"*.

Pauline, to Future Thin Me: *"Yes, I can be less greedy about eating, and I can see myself in the mirror and I'm pretty. I was able to reach my desired weight and go to the wedding in my party dress."*

T: *"What are some of the feelings you have as you look at the Future Thin Me?"*

P: *"Happiness, satisfaction, vanity"*

T: "*And on a scale of one to seven, where one is completely false and seven is completely true, how true does do these words, "I can control myself", feel to you when you look at her now?*" (VoC)

P: "*Four, five...*"

We did a few more bilateral movements (BLMs).

Pauline: "*Now that I think about it, I learned from my friends that when a person gains one or two pounds, that's the time to close your mouth and quit eating so much.*" (Here we see that the reprocessing has brought in new and positive content.)

T: "*Very well, and now how true do these words feel to you, 'I can control myself', as you look at the future on a scale of one to seven?*"

P: "*Five, five. But... I don't have any desire to return to the gym. I don't know how long I can take eating very little. I get up from the table feeling an empty sensation in my tummy, without feeling like I am full. That's when I feel like opening up a drawer and eating one of the chocolate bars.*"

Once again, we see progress in the reprocessing, but there continue to be obstacles to reaching the desired goal. The therapist uses another Cognitive Interweave to explore the possibility that there might be other roles in the Inner Gallery that are impeding progress.

T: "*I have the feeling that there is a little Ant[15] that lives inside of you as well... do you think?*"

Pauline: "*YES! I love sweets, just like the ants do!*"

T: "*Then choose a figure to represent the Ant.*"

Pauline chooses a big figure, tall with a hat, and places her in the *Play of Life* stage.

P: "*There is a little Ant that likes sweets. She says that chocolate is delicious, relaxing, and that it's wonderful to eat certain kinds of mousse... it's hard to resist... chocolate cake. At my house everyone eats dessert after lunch or dinner... we are used to it. I would have liked to have formed other habits... but I just LOVE a sweet after I finish eating.*"

T: "*Pauline, look at the size of the Ant.*"

---

[15] In Brazil, when people really like sweets they are referred to as "ants" because ants like sugar.

P: *"Yes... she's really big, isn't she? It's hard to even step on her."* (BLMs). *"But maybe if she went to sleep during the week and only woke up for a little bit on weekends?"* (BLMs). *"Give the Ant a sedative during the week and let her have just a little bite on weekends...?"*

T: *"And re-educate the Ant?"*

P: *"That's it! I can do that..."*

T: *"OK, then look again at the Future Thin Me. What do you perceive now?"*

P: *"I see myself in a picture taken at the wedding, in a picture frame, thin!"*

T: *"And on a scale of one to seven, where seven is completely true, how true to you feel these words to be now, "I can control myself"?"*

P: *"Now I think it's a seven. I am going to join the gym and spend more calories and that way I can eat sweets without stressing so much."*

T: *"Our time is coming to an end. Let's say goodbye to the figures on our stage? What would you like to say to them before you go?"*

P: *"I'm going to say to the Ant: 'you have to leave me alone for a while, at least during the week. I can control myself and have just a little bite of sweets. You have made me gain a lot of weight, instead of helping me lose it. I want to lose weight because it is also a health issue for me.'"*

Pauline to Fatty: *"Very soon you will be in my past!"*

Pauline to the Future Thin Me: *"You are going to become active again and will accompany me until I'm really old, and I will be pretty and healthy."*

Healing the Folks who Live Inside:
Why We Can Heal...

Now we have reached the part about how we can find ways to heal the Inner Gallery that lives within all of us. This chapter will not give all of the solutions and alternatives, but we hope that it will serve as a sufficiently clear map so that people can better understand what happens with our roles, our "statues of salt", our difficulties, in order for them to acquire a level of understanding and recovery that will give us a greater quality of life.

Before we embark on this great adventure, it is important to note that it is necessary to find somebody inside the Inner Gallery with enough commitment to health and sanity so as to form a therapeutic alliance with the other members of the Inner Gallery. If there is no internal commitment, there is no healing. Not all people are willing or capable of paying the price required for emotional healing.

Sometimes the terror of what people are "seeing" on the inside – old horror stories that continue to torment them in the present – prevent them from having the courage or the emotional resources to face their Inner Gallery. No one should feel guilty for this. All of us live the best we can. No one lives worse if they are able to live better. But not everybody seeks out a more functional way of living. As therapists, we need to understand that sometimes we need to let people live with their inner demons, their inner phantoms, even if this has a heavy price tag for them or for the people with whom they live. Not everyone wants to get well. We need to respect each person's limitations, even if it means that they live beneath their possibilities and potential.

It does happen – especially with therapists – that we want people to live with more - when they themselves prefer to live with less. But it isn't ethical to impose or require that clients live up to our standards of health and quality of life.

Therefore... for those who consider the option of living better, let's go to it!

1. **Who lives inside of me?** Many times we really don't know who lives inside. So the first step is to discover and identify who inhabits our Inner Gallery. If we pay attention, we can often hear the voices of those in our Inner Gallery. However, sometimes we need some outer help (like psychotherapy) to discover our inner inhabitants. Role therapy is especially useful, and the *Play of Life*™ kit possesses an extraordinary power to clarify these roles, as we saw in previous chapters.

Joan (a health food freak) came in one day, laughing all over the place and said: *"Last night I ate a bunch of junk food, and it really made me sick. I turned the light on inside and asked: 'Who was it in here that wanted to eat junk food?!'"*

2. Once inner roles are identified, **the healing process begins: finding ways to heal the hurt members of our Inner Gallery.** Many have splinters in their hearts and don't know where the emotional pain is coming from. It is important to hear what each role needs in order to heal. If we pay attention they will reveal their needs. This is not lunacy. It's just our inner roles speaking about their experiences. (In Psychodrama, this becomes even clearer as we put each role on the external stage and interview them.) Each one knows what happened and what it will take to get well, but sometimes it takes some special (professional) ability to help clarify the function of each role and the secret to their cure. They don't always give it up easily. It's interesting to note that sometimes what one role "knows" other ones do not.

Once, in a Psychodrama group therapy session, we were working on the roles of a university student. Everything was going pretty uneventfully as she was interviewed in all of her roles onstage, until she role-reversed with the person who was playing her father. Sandra, in her father's role, said with great concern, *"You know, I'm very worried about my daughter. Ever since her boyfriend died when she was 15, she has never gotten interested in another guy. Now she is 27 years old, and I'm concerned that she will never get married. I think she was traumatized by his death, since he was from a different country and she was too young to be allowed to go by herself to say good-bye to him."*

What Sandra didn't "know" in her adult role, her "inner father" knew and thus revealed the problem. This role knew that she would never marry unless she worked through this grief process that had gotten her stuck.

Another client mentioned that he had an Inner child that had been very affected by incidents in his childhood. This gentleman had gone through many troubles: a difficult and threatening father, and a childhood diagnosis that obliged him to go away from home very early for a long period of time in order to get treatment. He lived among strangers and couldn't remember his mother by the time he returned home. When I asked him what the Inner Child needed, he replied, *"I need to take care of this child, take him to the park to play. I'm going to buy him the little truck he always wanted but that my family was too poor to purchase for him. Now I have enough money to buy him nice toys and we are going to play together."* And for several months, he would shut himself in his bedroom and play with his trucks and cars until the day arrived when he no longer needed to do that. The child had received all of the love and affection he needed and could now leave that stage of development behind.

3. It is also important to understand that **we can't skip stages of development**. We can "compress time therapeutically" (go through stage in six months instead of six years), but there are some things that the members of our Inner Gallery need to go through (either internally in their imagination or externally as in the above example). These things need to be completed in chronological order, according to the developmental stages. We must be a child before we can be an adolescent. The truth is that our Inner Gallery is full of different roles with different ages (and some days they all talk at once!) Remember that day when you

went through a million different emotions, did incomprehensible things, picked a fight or got depressed without knowing why? And then at the end of the day you were exhausted?! Just imagine how many of these roles played havoc with us on that day...

Whenever possible, it is best to start healing the children first, since that is the order in which they appeared in our life.

4. At some point in the therapeutic process, **there needs to be a decision regarding who is "in charge" of my life and my Inner Gallery.** It doesn't make sense to go to work and let your Inner Child make decisions along with the boss. It's just not going to work! Once I told a patient that she needed to leave her inner children at the Kindergarten of Life so that she could behave like an adult at work. Children aren't supposed to go to work. They need to stay home and be cared for; otherwise they get in the way. When she got it, she was able to function much better at work, and she learned to deal with her boss in a more mature fashion.

5. **The Inner Gallery heals at the pace of the most fragile among them.** It is useless to try and overrun the process. When the people of Israel left Egypt, there were almost three million in total. They had sheep, goats, senior citizens, and women who had just had their babies. If the multitude had hurried along, the most fragile – humans and animals – would have died; or they would have been left behind to be devoured by savage animals or enemies. They would not have had access to water or food – essential in the desert. More than ever it was important to understand that these millions could only get out of that situation together but to do it, they had to travel at the pace of the most fragile. Sometimes it seems that the healing process is frustratingly slow, but being in a hurry can be fatal.

6. One of the biggest **problems our Inner Gallery members face is that of getting along together.** That is, they don't always know how to live in harmony. When one of the child roles takes over the driver's seat on this Trip of Life, problems happen. Children are not supposed to be driving! Driving is an adult role!

So, one of the aspects of getting well is healing our child roles so that everyone can live well together - one big happy family. Because the truth is that no one can be excused, thrown out, or mistreated without everyone suffering. When one member suffers, everyone does. Good or bad, everyone has to live together. It may be hell or it may be heaven, but it is going to be together. So negotiating good terms for harmonious living is an important part of healing.

For example, sometimes clients arrive at the office with internal conflicts. They want to quit smoking, lose weight or stop indulging in destructive behaviors. I tell them that there is someone in there who is not cooperating with the healthy option, and they have their reasons for it.

This "someone" likes to eat and does not have any interest in being deprived in order to lose weight. This "someone" likes smoking, especially when drinking a cup of coffee. And no matter how much the Adult in the picture argues with these roles, there is very little progress. Until patients can understand why they eat, or smoke or drink, "someone" is not going to give up his/her perceived pleasure. That's where the healing and negotiation phase has to occur.

7. **You can't kill inner roles.**

"There is a little six-year-old boy inside of me that hurts so much, so much, so much that I have tried to kill him many times by drinking or abusing drugs."

"Hey, there! If you kill him off, everybody inside dies, too."

The way out of this is healing and working it out so that the pain gets better, and everyone inside can live together with hurting each other. Many times people who contemplate suicide don't really want to die: they just want the pain to stop. It is better to heal than to die.

8. In this negotiating process we need to remember that sometimes **someone inside really did do things that the Adult**

felt was morally wrong. It may have been something that went against that person's own ethical or moral values. No matter how much you try to convince the adult that it's OK, that role knows that it's not. They know they did something wrong and need help with the negotiation process.

When we do something morally or ethically wrong happens, we respond in one of two ways: we either punish ourselves or we forgive. Many present-day behaviors have to do with self-chastisement for something that person did wrong in the past. Everyone is familiar with our Inner Tormentor. So, we can ask the person, *"What was it you did that was so serious that you do not deserve to be happy?"* Sometimes the answer shows us that it is false guilt and that the punishment is completely disproportionate to the alleged "crime." EMDR zaps false guilt, but true guilt has to be dealt with in another way.

When it is a matter of true guilt, then we need to ask what their sentence was when they were sent to Inner Jail. (You thought there wasn't a jail on the inside?) Oftentimes people don't know how to respond because they never gave themselves a sentence, only the judgment. So we ask, *"Is it a life sentence? You'll never be let out? How many years have you paid off already? How many years do you still have to pay off? Is it a death sentence and you are using some slow 'suicide' method like substance abuse?"* Questions like these help the person begin to realize that punishment is not always the best solution for those issues unless they are sure that one day they will be able to "get out." When criminals get out of jail they have paid off their debt to society.

But if punishment isn't the best solution, how do we deal with true guilt? That's where the issue of forgiveness comes in to the picture. It is important to learn to forgive the members of our Inner Gallery who did things which we did not condone. Forgiveness does not mean making believe it never happened- it means acknowledging that what was done was wrong. Instead of dealing with our inner members from a perspective of punishment, we can learn to relate to them (and/or others in the external world) through forgiveness; through reparation and reconciliation instead of the pain of resentment and bitterness. We will necessarily be relating to each other within our Inner Gallery all of our lives, but we can choose whether to do so through revenge (Shakespeare once said that revenge is like drinking poison and expecting the other to die) or forgiveness.

Forgiveness is a decision as well as a process. It means recognizing the enormity of what was done (or done against us) and even so, deciding to quit keeping accounts in the Accounting Book of Life. It means taking Life's Eraser and blotting out the outstanding accounts. It means that it is time to come out of the Inner Jail. Pardon has arrived.

9. **Perhaps the difference between acceptance and approval is not always perceived**. Many people say they will never "accept" such and such behavior – from inside or from outside – when, in truth, they mean they do not "approve" of it. Certain things happened and there is no way of changing the past. It is important to reach a point where one can accept the facts, but... not necessarily approve of them. We are not going to reach the point where we can approve of the idea that a husband went off with another woman, but we can learn to accept that this happened and that it cannot be changed. We will never approve of childhood sexual abuse (or abuse of any kind!), but we can accept that these things happen as part of the imperfect world (and people!) in which we live.

I once read (I can't remember where nor when) that a well-defined problem is half-solved. When we accept the fact that we were exposed to certain situations, we are "defining" the problem. Once the problem has been identified, that's when we can begin to seek out solutions.

10. **Consult the Inner Gallery**. One of the things that we can learn to do is to consult our Inner Gallery. All of us have a greater or lesser portion of inner wisdom that has come to us from experiences in life; from just going through stuff. Some people have an especially fine-tuned intuitive ability, but they do not trust what they feel or see or have learned.

Sometimes our learning process may have been distorted by the traumas of life, and as we heal these distortions we are more and more able to trust what we perceive.

For example, everybody has an Inner Doctor who seems to understand a lot about our illnesses. (The Outer Doctors complain a lot about the Inner Doctors of their patients because they often argue about diagnostics, meds and treatment!) When we have our doubts about what happens to us on the inside perhaps that is a good moment to consult our Inner Gallery. We might be surprised by their answers and their wisdom.

11. **We can also discard roles that no longer serve us.** This is another marvelous aspect of emotional recovery. As was mentioned before, health restores our ability to choose. As the members of our Inner Gallery heal, we can discard roles that no longer help us or that, in fact, have hindered us. We are not condemned to carry these roles forever. If they no longer help us we can throw them in Life's Great Trash Can.

That's it! I want to throw away all of these "emotional photographs" that have been in my Photo Book of Life, and keep only the good ones. The list is pretty long of things I want to get rid of, what "I Want" and "Don't Want", but there are a lot of things I would still like to keep. What comes to mind is fear... it has always been very present in my life, fear of making a mistake, of being successful, that won't let me move forward. But I think it's time to throw away the fear.

12. **On the other hand, we can acquire new roles.** I can develop new roles that will bring me more functionality and learn to be more adequate in my life. Instead of always picking a fight to get what I want, I can develop the Role of *Miss Good Manners* – the one who can make appropriate requests in an assertive and polite way. Or, I can learn the role of being happy; learn the good things of life. One of the best roles to learn is that of *Gratitude*. It is amazing how much everything changes when we are able to be grateful for what we have, instead of complaining about what we lack.

We can also "try on" new roles to see if they fit. Sometimes we'll find that new experiences are just great and we want more of them. Other times, however, we will discover that what we desired isn't for the best, and we can use our good common sense to not insist on going down that path. Not everything that is new is good.

13. Finally, **the past cannot be changed, but our perception of it can.** The facts will always be the same, but we can change. The members of our Inner Gallery can learn to have new perspectives about what happened. Instead of thinking that we will be forever marked by tragedy, or disaster or terror, we can change our perspective so that the past loses its power to harm us. We can melt our statues of salt and become human.

The Inner Gallery Speaks: Mary Anne's Session

What follows are significant portions from Mary Anne's session. She was born in China and lived through the radical transformation of her country under the communist regime of Mao Tse-Tung. Several members of her family were victims of the cruelty of this newly established regime. As a child, Mary Anne saw her grandfather executed before her eyes. Other family members died of hunger. China was so dangerous that her parents found a way to flee to Brazil, but their children, including Mary Anne, had to stay behind. Mary Anne's parents hoped that by establishing themselves in a new country they would be able to bring their children to live with them, which eventually did happen.

Mary Anne was raised by her grandparents and an aunt, but when she went to live in Brazil, she found her parents very traumatized by what they had gone through, and incapable of showing love or acceptance. Oftentimes her father would have rage attacks, and expel the children from home. On one of these occasions, Mary Anne left for good. She had some friends who helped her, initially giving her a place to live, and later even paying for her studies in this foreign country so that she could become a psychologist. Years later, she got married, but the marriage ended, and her husband left her with three small children to raise on her own. Mary Anne was able to overcome all of these obstacles, but she wound up dealing with a lot of depression and anxiety for no apparent cause. She couldn't find a good reason to stay alive. She came to this session with many of these issues fairly resolved due to previous therapy work, which is why she asked if she could do a "light" session this time around. Mary Anne said that she didn't have the emotional energy to deal with the dragons from her past.

In this session, the therapist used several positive interventions with the goal of informing her inner roles that the danger was past, and that Mary Anne had made it in life. Since Mary Anne spoke several foreign languages and her memories were connected to what had happened in different phases of her life, the therapist had to take this into consideration in the reparative work that follows. Here we see how we can use present-day information to instruct past roles with the goal of placing the past in the past, and structuring the present in positive terms.

Since this was a complete EMDR session, we offer a limited amount of information to the EMDR therapists that will read this report. In a previous session, Mary Anne had described many of the details regarding her pain, especially what she had lived through and seen by the time she was five years old. So the present starting point for integrating her past roles was the earliest one, that of Mary Anne Child.

Therapist (T): *"Mary Anne, today I would like for you to pay attention to that Little Mary Anne who saw so much tragedy by the time she was five years old. Describe how you see her now."*

Mary Anne (M): *"Well, I have brought her to live with me in my home, where I live now. So I see her in my house today."*

T: *"And when you think about this, what do you think about yourself that is negative, false and irrational?"*

M: *"I am abandoned."* (Negative cognition)

T: *"And if I had a magic wand, what would you like to think about yourself now that is positive regarding this experience?"*

M: *"That I am strong, that I have people who love me."*

T: *"And on a scale of one to seven, where seven is completely true and one is completely false, how true do you feel these positive words to be regarding this experience?"*

M: *"I feel that it is a seven; that I am strong."*

T: *"When you think of this picture of you in your home with Mary Anne Child, what emotions do you feel?"*

M: *"Sadness."*

T: *"On a scale of zero to ten, where zero means no disturbance at all, and ten is the highest amount of disturbance that you can imagine, how much disturbance do you feel now regarding this experience?"*

M: *"Six."*

T: *"And where do you feel that in your body?"*

M: *"In my heart. I feel the palpitations."*

T: *"OK. Mary Anne, today we are going to do things a bit differently. Since your Little Girl lives with you now in your home, I think we need to let her know about some things about which she may not be aware. This little five-year-old only knows how to speak Chinese, right? What is her Chinese name?"*

M: *"An-yon."*

T: *"Very well. While I do some bilateral movements, I would like for you to speak to An-Yon in Chinese, since she doesn't know how to speak Portuguese."*

M: *"That's true!!!"*

T: *"Speak to her in Chinese and tell her that she no longer lives in China and that now she lives with you. Show her the new house where she lives, and explain everything to her, since children get scared when they don't understand what is happening to them."*

M: *"Very well."*

Mary Anne closed her eyes while the therapist did tactile bilateral movements. All of a sudden, in a very soft voice, Mary Anne began to speak in a Chinese dialect, which she hadn't spoken in many, many years. After a few minutes of speaking this way, Mary Anne opened her eyes and said:

M: *"I spoke to An-Yon, and I showed her my house: her new bedroom, the decorations that I brought with me from my last trip to china a few years ago. I explained to her that here she is protected, and that I will take good care of her. I have my own home now and I have enough money to care for both of us. So now An-Yon can be a child. She can play, have fun and enjoy herself. She can go to school and I, Mary Anne Adult, will take care of her. An-Yon was very happy about this!"*

T: *"That is beautiful! You know, when we leave a place, a country, we leave many bad things behind, like An-Yon. But there were also good things, and good people. I would like for you to imagine that there is a magic window in your house and that for a few minutes, through the window An-Yon can see that China she left. Have her look and see if there is anything there that she would like to bring to her new house with her. Since today An-Yon only exists inside of you, she can bring whoever she wants to live with you, obviously, if ya'll are in agreement."*

Mary Anne closed her eyes once again, and spoke in Chinese while the therapists did a few more tactile bilateral movements. After a few minutes, Mary Anne opened her eyes and said:

M: *"We brought my grandparents to come and live with us, and an aunt that cared for me and loved me very much. An-Yon showed them her bedroom, and I told them that they would stay with us. I told them what had happened to me during all of these years, that now I am a recognized psychologist, and – I took them to see my consulting office! They were very proud of me! All of us are so happy that the nightmare is over, and that now we can all live together. I used to feel very lonely in my apartment, but look at how many people live there now!"*

T: (Very moved). *"It seems there's no reason to be so depressed about being lonely, right? There are a lot of good people living with you now!"*

T: *"Who else do we need to inform that now you live in this pretty apartment, that you have a home, your own money, your profession?"*

M: *"My 13-year-old adolescent. At this point, I already lived in Brazil. I was able to get out of China. I can speak Portuguese by now, but my parents are very difficult. My mother would say terrible things to me, just horrible! And my father would kick me out of the house. This young person is very angry."*

T: *"So, let's tell Mary Anne Adolescent how the story ends?"*
M: *"Yes!"*

And once again, Mary Anne closed her eyes while the therapist did tactile bilateral movements. Now Mary Anne spoke in Portuguese, and talked about her apartment and invited her Adolescent to come and live with her in her present-day life.

M: *"I showed another bedroom to Mary Anne Adolescent, where she would live with me. You know, adolescents like to have their own space. I told her everything, including who we had become. She was very happy about it. She told me that she could understand that her mother had a very difficult life, that her parents were complicated, that she had suffered very much, and that she had been unable to be a better mother. The truth was that her mother (my grandmother), died when my mother was only ten years old... there were moments when my own mother wanted to kill me... my mother suffered very much when she had to leave her children behind in China in order to escape Communism. She knew that her children would suffer a lot as well under the new regime, until she was able to bring them to Brazil... but now I understand what she* went through. It was really, really hard. She did the best she could and the Adolescent isn't mad at her anymore."

T: "Very well... who else on the inside needs to know about your present-day success?"

M: "Hmm... the Divorced Mother. She was only 36 years old, and had a lot of financial burdens, because there were three small children, and she didn't know how she was going to pay the bills... how she was going to educate them."

T: "So, let's tell her how you have overcome these circumstances, that the children are already grown up, and that all have been able to get a privileged education and are doing well in life?"

M: "OK." (Mary Anne closes her eyes while the therapist does tactile bilateral movements.) "Ah, I showed her the photographs of my grown children. Each one has their own profession. They're married and are beginning to have children. My children said to her that she doesn't need to be concerned about them anymore, because when she retires, they want to take care of her – that they want to take care of her! I showed her the pictures of my grown children."

T: "So, do you think she can relax and think about the future?"

M: "Yes... but I'm very afraid of the future... of not having a good reason to live for, of getting depressed, of being alone, lonely, of not having good health..."

T: "Well, how about we look at the future with what you have accomplished today? What do you have now that can help you face the future?"

M: "I no longer live in China! That is an enormous relief! I'm no longer in danger. I don't live with a father who kicks me out of the house. You know, one day he did that and I decided I would never go back. A wonderful friend helped me study and become a professional. She paid for my studies, can you imagine that? We are still friends to this day... I have a lot of good friends... and that is very good! I have my own house, where no one can expel me. I have my own money... I'm not rich, but I have enough to live on and I know that I will not lack. I have a good reputation in my profession and highly regarded. Other professionals send me their patients because they trust my work. I am proud of who I have become professionally... that's right! I have a lot! I have a lot!"

T: "So, what's your life like now?"

M: "Ah, there are a lot of good people in my house. There's An-

Yon, my Adolescent, the Divorced Mother that can rest from her tasks now; my grandparents, my aunt... there are a lot of people living in my house! I'm not alone! I'm no longer helpless!"

T: *"So, now that you know that there are so many wonderful people living with you and that you have a secure future, what are the positive words that you would like to connect to this experience?"*

M: *"I'm strong."*

T: *"On a scale of one to seven where seven is completely true and one is completely false, how true do you feel these words to be, I am strong, when you think about this experience now?"*

M: *"Seven.* (The therapist does a few bilateral movements to install the positive cognition.)*"*

T: *"Let's check some other cognitions? How about, I have people who love me and care for me?"*

M: *"Seven."* (The therapist does a few bilateral movements to install the positive cognition.)

T: *"I am courageous?"* (The client had talked about not being courageous earlier in the session.)

M: *"Seven."* (The therapist does a few bilateral movements to install the positive cognition.)

T: *"I have my own home?"*

M: *"Seven."* (The therapist does a few bilateral movements to install the positive cognition.)

T: *"I have my own money?"*

M: *"Seven."* (The therapist does a few bilateral movements to install the positive cognition.)

T: *"I have people who can help me?"*

M: *"Seven."* (The therapist does a few bilateral movements to install the positive cognition.)

T: *"I have my own space?"*

M: *"Eight!!"* And laughs... (The therapist does a few bilateral movements to install the positive cognition.)

T: *"I have a good future?"*

M: *"Hmm, five, five... I am afraid of becoming helpless, and that no one will care for me."*

T: *"Let's go with that and follow my movements."* (The therapist does a few reprocessing bilateral movements too.)

M: *"I have my children who will care for me and never allow me* to lack for anything. I don't want to be a burden to them, but I know I am not helpless. I even have grandchildren who are becoming young adults and they like me, and even say they want to care for me. So, yes, I am cared for. It's seven."

T: "*Ok, think about that.*" (The therapist does a few bilateral movements to install the positive cognition.)

T: "*So, let's finalize our session. You have such beautiful work and need to be proud of yourself. You have overcome so many challenges in live, so many tragedies, but you no longer live in those situations of suffering. That is over forever. Now you have you own home, your own money, many good friends, wonderful children who care for you, and have this whole Inner Gallery on the inside that lives with you in your apartment. You are not alone! You are a person whose life has worked out for good.*"

In this session, we can see how we can use EMDR applied as role therapy in a reparative function. Here Mary Anne was able to create a whole new positive world on the inside, let go of old tragedies from the past, and learn to enjoy all that she has attained. Perhaps psychotherapy oftentimes emphasizes what goes wrong in life and people work on that. However, sometimes it is important to emphasize what "goes right" so that people can develop a greater measure of hope for their lives. Having overcome so many obstacles in her life, it important that Mary Anne be able to communicate all of this to her inner roles – the roles who had not yet received all of the good news regarding what she had accomplished with her life. EMDR not only helps to "unfreeze" the roles, but it also helps to develop a new internal perspective – and a positive one – about how life can be better.

A few days later, Mary Anne sent me an e-mail:

Two nights after our session, I dreamed that I was in a hospital trying to care for a child. Then I saw myself in the house of a childhood friend with whom I am still friends. She is about the same age as I am, is single and lives alone. At a certain point in my adolescence, my last year of high school, my father kicked me out of the house, in one of his rage attacks, like I told you. This friend was present when it happened...

So... back to the dream, I was very anxious because I was so busy I couldn't finish cooking the meal for some poor children who were waiting for me in a bus to take them for a fun time. But a lady arrived and helped me finish cooking the meal and I was able to get together with the children for the meal.

I'm telling you this dream so that you can have an idea of how integrating our session was. I see in my dream that I can feed all of these hungry and deprived children (my inner roles in the session that we were able to heal and repair) even though I was late because I was so busy, which would often happen when I was older. I was surprised with this dream... it was so illuminating.

All of us send you our best regards, Afui, the niece of An-Yon, and Mary Anne.

In Conclusion...

We hope that it has been possible to explain who comprise our Inner Gallery and how we can learn to have a better living relationship with those roles who live inside of us. Perhaps there are people who, having read this, will seek an opportunity to seek the help they need. The truth is that psychotherapy is not just for crazy people. It is for people who have an Inner Gallery with roles that are rebellious, upset, scared and traumatized; and who would like to negotiate their process of healing and recovery. It is our desire that this book may bring a good dose of hope: that we don't have to live trapped in our past experiences, but that as we better understand what happened to us, we might heal. We can look at a new future with new opportunities and choices. We have shared little pieces of others' stories, those who have gone through this process, so that we can illustrate how this psychotherapeutic perspective works. Perhaps in the near future we will put out a book with more complete stories and case histories.

I hope that you have enjoyed the pilgrimage through the corridors of the Inner Gallery as well as the Outer Gallery (those in others!), and that you may come to believe in the power of EMDR to heal our own inner roles. Hopefully, you will be able to find experienced therapists whose love and empathy will help melt the salt statues of past terror with which you may be familiar yourself.

About the Author

Esly Regina Carvalho, Ph.D, is a Brazilian-American clinical psychologist, EMDR Trainer of Trainers (EMDR Institute and EMDR Iberoamérica); president EMDR Entrenamiento e Consultoria Ltda., the organization that offers basic training in Brazil; president of EMDR Ibero-América (EMDR IBA, 2007-2010 and 2010-2013). Esly was approved *with distinction* as a Trainer, Educator, Practitioner (TEP) by the American Board of Examiners in Psychodrama, Sociometry and Group Psychotherapy. She is a *Fellow* of American Society of Group Psychotherapy and Psychodrama (ASGPP); the founder and honorary member of the Asociación de Psicodrama y Sociometría del Ecuador (APSE). Esly is a native speaker of Portuguese and English, and is very fluent in Spanish. She is an international presenter in great demand and the author of several books in these three languages. She presently offers training in this new modality, integrating EMDR with role therapy.

Esly Regina Carvalho, Ph.D.

Contact information:
www.plazacounselingservices.com
info@plazacounselingservices.com

Made in the USA
San Bernardino, CA
28 May 2016